feeling like God

the emotional side of discipleship—and why you can't fully follow Jesus without it

chris tiegreen

SALT**RIVER**®

AN IMPRINT OF
TYNDALE HOUSE PUBLISHERS, INC.
Carol Stream, Illinois

Visit Tyndale's exciting Web site at www.tyndale.com

Visit Chris Tiegreen's Web site at www.christiegreen.com

TYNDALE is a registered trademark of Tyndale House Publishers, Inc.

SaltRiver and the SaltRiver logo are registered trademarks of Tyndale House Publishers, Inc.

Feeling like God: The Emotional Side of Discipleship—and Why You Can't Fully Follow Jesus without It

Designed by Jessie McGrath

Edited by Karin Stock Buursma

Published in association with the literary agency of Mark Sweeney & Associates.

Library of Congress Cataloging-in-Publication Data

Tiegreen, Chris.
    Feeling like God : the emotional side of discipleship and why you can't fully follow Jesus without it / Chris Tiegreen.
        p. cm.
    Includes bibliographical references.
    ISBN-13: 978-1-4143-1565-2 (sc)
    ISBN-10: 1-4143-1565-1 (sc)
    1. Christian life. 2. Emotions—Religious aspects—Christianity. I. Title.
BV4501.3.T54 2008
248.4—dc22   2007050711

Printed in the United States of America

14   13   12   11   10   09   08
 7   6   5   4   3   2   1

CONTENTS

LOVE ALONE KNOWS what it was like before all time began, when the fellowship of three conceived a dream to share its joy. This cosmic dance was opened up with perfect, pure delight—a gladness that was never born but always very alive. As yet, no sacred veil would interfere to hide these feelings streaming long and deep, as intimate secrets flowed at will from Father to Son to Spirit to Son to Father and back again through each—a never-ending circle in a rhythmic celebration. Like brightly glowing embers that burn with growing fervor, they could satisfy each other yet were always seeking more. Unhindered in intensity, such passion can't resist the urge to burst out in its pleasure and invite all those who listen to come drink of its sweet beauty, and then charm all those who taste it to be captive to its love. "What music would our voices sing if breathing through another—like us . . . but *not* us; with us . . . but *in* us; and always where we are?" Relentless holy union for the first time skipped a beat, and this glory-driven circle stirred with new creative songs and broke the silence of its kingdom with a blessing on its dream:

> *"Let us make them in our image,*
> *let our heart be multiplied!*
> *If we breathe the breath of romance*
> *into dust and ask it to dance,*
> *we can gaze forever into souls*
> *invited to our ball."*

Perfectly good, creation gasped, and so the world began. Now carefully formed by the breath of the three, never before was an image so true—and lovingly primed to know the joy of the heartbeat of its King.

mysteries of his heart

the emotional side of God

THE OPENING SCENES of the movie *A River Runs Through It* depict a Presbyterian father training his two sons in the deep spiritual lessons of life and fly-fishing. Because he believes life is set in motion and sustained by God's unwavering rhythms, Reverend Maclean teaches his boys to discern the order of creation and to cast their lines by the cadence of a metronome. God's word, he tells them, lies underneath layers of rock a half-billion years old, and if they listen carefully, they might hear it. Creation is filled with laws, rules, and principles: the steady pace of the clock, the ethics of an honest living, an ever-reliable river, diligent study and prayer—and, most of all, ʌts necessary to keep sinful souls in line. Even artistry ... Life is all about order.

This father's instruction in reading and writing is stern and pointed, and his affirmation is always carefully measured. There is love in this minister's home, but it's only implied. It's the unstated reason behind the sons' lessons in methods and discipline, as well as the source of their freedom to spend their afternoons fishing. Much like a sermon the reverend preaches—a staid, eloquent homily on the deepest feelings of the heart, given while standing under a bland wooden panel behind the pulpit that's carved with the words, "God is love"—emotions are theoretically legitimate. But they are never practiced, never even discussed, except in the most serious terms. Apparently, acknowledging their existence is acceptable. Being drawn into their influence seems unwise.

Two telling scenes near the end of the movie capture the emotional flavor of the family. In one, Reverend Maclean can hardly contain his pride when Norman, the older son, is offered a university teaching position. So how does this proud father let his feelings flow? "Well," he says, struggling to control his smile, "I am pleased. . . . I *am* pleased." A few scenes later, when Norman has to tell his parents that his brother was found dead in an alley—a victim of his own reckless living—his mother slowly and shakily rises without saying a word and then stumbles up the stairs into privacy. The father asks a few somber questions, but his face remains unaffected. Among these stunned family members, there are no wails, no sobs, no tears. Not even any hugs. From their greatest expressions of pleasure to their deepest horrors of grief, their dignity is ever maintained.[1]

In contrast, Colonel Christopher Brandon feels emotions deeply and, at times, wears them openly. This honorable gentleman from

Jane Austen's *Sense and Sensibility* [2] falls deeply in love with the young Marianne Dashwood—an expressive, temperamental girl who reminds him of his first love years before. That long-ago love ended tragically, and Brandon is clearly still tormented by its sorrow. Now face-to-face with another young woman of "impulsive sweetness," his passion swells again. Rising, falling, pleading, wishing, his love is torn between two destinies: too realistic to soar on the winds of hope, too desperate to crash on the rocks of circumstance. He's reluctant to dream, and reluctant not to dream—trapped in romantic purgatory.

Brandon's affections are obvious to those who are observant, but Marianne either doesn't notice them or intentionally ignores them. Instead, she falls head over heels for the dashing John Willoughby, who seems equally enamored of her. Colonel Brandon watches in silent anguish as the romance between his true love and her handsome suitor develops. His heartbroken eyes grieve every affectionate glance between Marianne and Willoughby, who makes fun of him when he's not around. The beautiful flowers he gives her get pushed aside to make room for her boyfriend's cheap bouquet. The characteristics Brandon loves about Marianne—she's the passionate, sentimental "sensibility" from the title—are the same characteristics that drive her toward this charming man she knows little about. And every day, Brandon aches from the sight.

In spite of Marianne's blind devotion to another man, the colonel's love for her never wavers. He knows her fleeting passion will lead to heartache; Willoughby's an irresponsible cad who will never deserve her. But affections can't be forcibly turned from the directions they've chosen, so Brandon keeps his silence. When Marianne is distraught over Willoughby's callous treatment of her, Brandon tries to ease her pain by explaining the dirty truth behind the actions of her unworthy beau—how his immoral behavior would have eventually led to heartbreak anyway. When she needs rescuing in a storm, he finds her in a field overlooking the mansion where Willoughby and his new, wealthy wife now live, and he carries her three miles in driving rain. And when her life is threatened by an infectious fever, he paces constantly, consumed with concern and desperate for anything that will help her. He is faithful to the love of his heart, even though her heart has run in another, self-destructive direction.

A MULTIPLE CHOICE QUESTION

Between those two pictures—a devout, dignified minister and father, and a passionate romantic in the throes of heartbreak—which is biblically closer to the personality of God? Is he compassionate but reserved? Or does he wear his heart on his sleeve? Are his emotions carefully measured by the laws of the universe and the rhythms of creation, or do they bleed into the soil of human sin? According to his own revelation, what is God's emotional makeup? Is he happy? angry? sad? complacent? Is he ever in a good mood?

Are God's emotions carefully measured by the laws of the universe and the rhythms of creation, or do they bleed into the soil of human sin?

In the minds of most people, God is a lot like Reverend Maclean. Love is there, but it is a formal and willful love. It's the kind of love a family has for its most difficult member: obligatory when it's essential, but never a delight. It's something to rely on and to break your fall in an emergency, but if you want to see it in the normal course of life, you have to look for it. It's the never-changing river that runs through our stories—present but unspeaking, consistent but unaffected by those who stand on its banks, always moving but never moved. That kind of implied love may be a reassuring assumption in a crisis, but it doesn't make for a great relationship.

The Bible far more often describes God as an emotionally charged being who is deeply, relentlessly in love with his people and who interacts with them regularly on that basis. The story of Colonel Brandon's faithful love in the face of rejection is a tragic picture of human heartbreak, but it's not a far cry from the prophets' portrayal of God's feelings when Israel jilted him for worthless idols. God's epic romance is filled with twists and turns of hopefulness, irony, and grief. And, like Brandon, he will ultimately get his bride in the end. Stories of human love are often necessarily different than stories of God's love, as God doesn't experience the same kind of desperation we do. But they aren't as different as we often think. God, according to his own revelation, is subject to extremes of passion.

It's true that God's ways and thoughts are inexpressibly higher than our ways and thoughts,³ which is why theologians have a difficult time with his emotions. How *would* an infinite being feel? Our Father is not surprised by anything, so he doesn't feel the shock of tragedy or boil over in sudden outrage. He's too wise and powerful to be governed by whims, moods, and the ups and downs of everyday life in heaven. He's all-knowing and all-powerful, perfectly loving and perfectly understanding, and nothing catches him off guard. So he doesn't feel exactly the same emotions we would feel in a given situation. That changes somewhat in the incarnation; though Jesus has the same emotions as the Father, they are filtered through human eyes and experiences. But those feelings are still the perfect image of God's heart. And his thoughts—and feelings—are higher and holier than ours.

At the same time, we're also made in his image, which means there must be at least *some* correspondence between our makeup and his. The couple he placed in the garden was crafted to be a picture of his likeness. And even though that picture was vandalized by the first sin, the goal of creation is still to have an image of God on earth reflecting who he is. That's why we are being made into the likeness of Christ—to restore and perfect God's image in creation. We're designed to be a visible representation of our Maker. So it stands to reason that we would learn not only to think like him and to act like him but also to *feel* like him. We are destined to share every aspect of his personality.

How do we reconcile the constancy of divine love and joy with the ups and downs of feelings and moods? After all, it just isn't logical for attributes of an unchanging God to mix with volatile human frailties. And we certainly want a God who fits our logic, don't we? So most Christian theology ascribes deep emotional qualities to God without "humanizing" those emotions. We are comfortable as long as he has the "good" feelings—love, joy, peace, compassion, delight—in unchanging permanence; and we are nervous when we talk about the dynamics of his anger and grief. We can acknowledge these attributes, but we sterilize them. We know they have to be different than ours because we know what ours are really like: fickle, misplaced, and distorted by misperceptions and sin.

> We're designed to be a visible representation of our Maker. So it stands to reason that we would learn not only to think like him and to act like him but also to feel *like him.*

Because of our experience with emotions—either our own or someone else's—we try to distance God from them. We know he isn't fickle or out of control, so therefore, we reason, he can't be emotional. But defining God's personality by our own experience will take us pretty far off track. Flawed human beings are never an accurate picture of divine truth. They simply shape our perspective, usually negatively. That explains why the American evangelical mind-set often uses words like *emotions*, *feelings*, and *heart* as evidence of spiritual immaturity. They are associated with extremes like rage and despondency or, at the very least, instability. That's just too human to mix with God.

But we forget: The attributes of an unchanging God *did* mix with volatile human frailties during one particular lifetime. We call him Immanuel, God with us, the incarnation of the Holy One himself. If we ever wondered how to reconcile the ups and downs of moods with the constancy of God, all we have to do is look at Jesus. We know he's the exact representation of God,[4] and we also know he never sinned.[5] Yet he got angry, he grieved, and he cried out with a loud voice and tears.[6] For godly emotions, that looks remarkably human.

According to Scripture, God experiences nearly the full range of emotions that human beings feel, with a few exceptions we'll discuss later. And his feelings are presented in pretty subjective terms, not as static attributes that fit our idea of holiness. He loves, hates, rejoices, grieves, is zealous, gets jealous, and swells in anger when his mission is obstructed or his character impugned. And, according to his own Word, God is not immune to heartbreak.

GODLY GRIEF

In fact, heartbreak is the most prominent emotion of God in the prophetic books. If he were simply disappointed in his people or angry over how badly they'd messed up, he would express only judgment and wrath. In fact, that's what many people see in the God of Israel in the Old Testament: plenty of wrath with an occasional hint of grace. And if Reverend Maclean represents our perception of God—with restrained and unchanging affections—it's no wonder his dealings with Israel seem harsh and unbalanced. But underlying every incident of God's wrath toward his own people is their betrayal of his love. He gets angry in Scripture not because he likes to or because that's his natural disposition, but because he has so lavishly poured out his affections and they've been thrown back in his face again and again. That's why God repeatedly inspired his prophets to use the image of an abandoned husband whose precious bride has prostituted herself. God doesn't come across in Scripture as angry at impersonal objects. He comes across as a lover who's been stabbed in the back.

That image is perhaps clearest in the book of Hosea, which tells of a prophet who not only had to tell God's message but live it. While many of us get to live the upside of God's message—the joy that flows in and out of a harmonious, passionate marriage—Hosea's calling was to portray God's heartbreak by marrying a prostitute who kept abandoning her loving husband to sleep with other men. That's not the sort of call that most of us dream of receiving from God, but in this case someone has to do it. Why? Because God wants a visible, graphic illustration of repeated forgiveness for repeated betrayal, and a visual explanation to show why he would have to separate himself from his beloved people. For an excruciating season, Hosea and God shared the same heart.

Hosea lived the pain of God's emotions, but Ezekiel described them perhaps even more vividly. Chapter 16 of his book offers what may be the most jolting picture of betrayal in Scripture. Israel is portrayed as an abandoned baby girl still squirming in afterbirth in an open field. God, in his great compassion, took her in, clothed her, raised her, and beautified her. When she became "old enough for love" (v. 8, NIV), he brought her into a more intimate relationship with him. He treated her like a queen—doted on her, gave her expensive gifts, lavished his love and his wealth on her.

Realizing how beautiful he had made her, she showed her gratitude by becoming a prostitute and sleeping with whatever lowlife she could find. All of the clothing and jewelry he had so extravagantly given her became the currency of her adultery; instead of receiving gifts from her lovers, she paid them for the privilege of her promiscuity. And then, to top it all off, she took the children born from the intimate marriage with her faithful husband and slaughtered them—burned them at the feet of idols. She had been given the treasures of heaven, and what did she do? Traded them in for poisons and pain.

That kind of imagery doesn't come from a God who's beyond the sway of passions. It comes from someone whose heart can be broken; who hurts when his love is unrecognized, thwarted, and abused; and who even told his beloved people that his name was Jealous.[7] He didn't just warn them that he might be *prone* to jealousy. No, he said it defined him—or at least a part of his true character. This high and holy God who, according to theologians, is far above the ups and downs of human emotion, sometimes smolders, even burns, with the jealousy of a jilted lover.[8]

How do we reconcile this scriptural picture of God with our theological belief in his "immutability"? After all, the fact that he is unchanging is scriptural too.[9] The distinction is that fluctuating emotions do not imply a change in personality or in essence. God is always God, and his essence never changes. However, God's immutability does not make him a static deity. In Scripture, when people interact with him on issues of his will, he changes directions.[10] Yet his ultimate purposes and his eternal personality are not altered. We don't contradict God's unchanging nature when we talk about his emotions coming and going.

God is also unlike us in his capacity to feel multiple emotions at once. We do this to a degree when, for example, we weep at someone's funeral even though we're glad he or she is done with suffering and is now in the presence of God. We call that "mixed feelings." But God has mixed feelings all the time. At this very moment, for instance, God is comforting someone who's hurting, feeling anger at someone's stubborn rebellion, rejoicing over a sinner who just repented, delighting in the prayers of his children, grieving over the tragedies we inflict on ourselves, and remaining at perfect peace about his plans for the world. In finite beings like us, we'd call that "conflicted" and go in for counseling. In an infinite God, however, multiple emotions are normal.

This is one reason the "God never changes" argument against his emotional constitution is unfounded. It's based on our experience with our own emotions, which we usually feel in succession rather than simultaneously. With God, that's not an issue. Though his emotions do, in fact, change in Scripture, they don't change suddenly and dramatically like ours do. He doesn't leave joy behind when he grieves or forget his anger against Satan while he's rejoicing over those who have come to him in faith. When God leaves anger behind, as he does when separating us from our sins at the Cross, it's because he chooses to, not because another emotion comes along and replaces it by filling up the only space he has in his heart. God's unchanging personality feels a lot of different things in a lot of different places at the very same time. He is always moving and never stilled by the status quo. It is in his unchanging nature to be dynamic.

As a result, we find the always-beating, sometimes-bleeding heart of God on nearly every page of Scripture if we look closely enough. He feels the same ways we do—not because we've made God in our image, as some suggest, but because he made us in his.

A DEEPER CONNECTION

Why is this important? Because God calls us into a relationship with him. To know God is more than to acknowledge his characteristics and describe his attributes. To know him is to bond with him and to grow continually deeper in our connection with him. That can't be done apart from emotions. We don't connect with people through shared information or even shared experiences. Have you, for example, bonded with all those people you spent long hours with in a driver's license renewal line who were waiting for the same experience you were about to have? Or come out of a lengthy budget meeting strongly attached to people you've shared a lot of information with? Probably not. Shared information and experiences in themselves don't draw us closer. It's the shared emotional responses to that information and experience that creates closeness. When our sentiments line up with someone else's, we feel a connection. When they don't, we don't. That's how a mutual bond develops.

To know God is to bond with him and to grow continually deeper in our connection with him. That can't be done apart from emotions.

But the church today too often focuses on the establishment of the relationship (salvation) and the factual basis of the relationship (Bible study) to the exclusion of cultivating the relationship (emotional responses). There's nothing wrong with emphasizing evangelism and discipleship—thank God for those who have done so—but when we simultaneously do all we can to chase emotions out of those aspects of the relationship, we're missing the whole point. Salvation and study are the means to an end—"pleasures forevermore," according to Psalm 16:11[11]—not the end in themselves. God didn't create us to "get saved." He saves us so we can know him and relate to him in every facet of our personalities, including (or especially) emotionally. But we're so focused on getting "truth" right in all its details that we miss the joy that the truth is supposed to lead to.

As a result, we have plenty of vehicles that can get people on the path to growth, but no fuel to help those vehicles go anywhere. We're great with the road map, but we usually just hand it to people and send them on a business trip to meet with God. And no one really wants to linger very long on a business trip.

God really enjoys mixing business and pleasure. He likes the informational meetings we have with him—they're very important—but he loves the leisure time more. His ultimate goal is for us to rest in his presence and to experience his joy—the "room temperature" of heaven. Most of all, he wants us to connect with him. That's why he created us; he wants to share his Spirit with us. And his Spirit, wherever he shows up in Scripture, always prompts some sort of emotional response.

The implications of that are huge. If God is a thoroughly emotional being, we can't really get to know him unless we know the emotions he feels, no matter how much objective truth we've learned. And we can't really *know* the emotions he feels unless we experience them. (Consider that next time you're suffering from heartbreak. You're feeling the same way he feels when his people break his heart. Kind of makes his character come alive in your experience, doesn't it?) In order to get to know our sentient God better, we have to be sensitive to the emotions he expresses in Scripture.

The importance of sharing his emotions shows up often in Scripture, but Jesus' comments in Revelation to the seven churches are particularly revealing. He gave them specific encouragement as well as specific rebukes. The Ephesian church, for example, got high marks for doctrinal purity and enduring patiently in the face

His Spirit, wherever he shows up in Scripture, always prompts some sort of emotional response.

of persecution. So why would Jesus have anything negative to say to that congregation? Well, they had lost their first love. That's it. And he told them to repent.[12] Likewise, the church at Sardis was rebuked for being dead rather than alive and urged to do works that better exemplify a church with energy and love.[13] They had the truth, and they did some good works, but there was no life in them. Finally, the well-known church at Laodicea had the distinction of nauseating the Lord because of their lukewarmness.[14] In love and practice they were neither hot nor cold, and that was revolting to God.

Some of the churches in Asia Minor were rebuked because they weren't lined up with God's truth or his work, but it's also clear that some were rebuked because they were not lined up with his heart. Why? Because they had let their love grow cold, their energy and motivation die, and their complacency and apathy lead them astray. They weren't vitally and meaningfully connected with their Savior at points that mattered deeply to him.

It's clear that God has a lot of emotional expectations for his people. Why? Because he's very emotional himself. He has a dynamic personality that feeds emotional responses and receives them wholeheartedly.

Far from giving us feelings as a fringe benefit, he established them in us as core elements of our personhood. He wants our hearts to swell and to soar with his.

Reverend Maclean is right about the universe operating on a rhythm, but he is wrong about the nature of the beat. It isn't uniform and impersonal. The world isn't filled with principles and order for the sake of principles and order; it was fashioned according to the heartbeat of a God who feels. His pulse was dictating the days of creation, his joy rising up with every "It was good." He took great pleasure in each new masterpiece, and he crowned his pleasure with beings made to feel the way he feels.

CHAPTER 2

why vulcans miss the best part

knowing and doing isn't enough

I GREW UP AS an avid fan of the Atlanta Braves, which may explain my inferiority complex better than a century of counseling ever could. Those familiar only with the Braves' recent history won't understand that statement, but for the first couple of decades of my life, the Braves were bad. *Real* bad. A synonym for futility—as in, "Of course that guy's home on Friday night; he strikes out almost as often as the Braves do." Or, "What do the inmates at the state pen and the Atlanta Braves have in common? They got caught stealing." My little league team would echo a familiar lament after every loss: "Man, we played so bad we would've only beat the Braves by five runs." It was rough.

But in 1991, that changed. The Braves went from last place in the league in 1990 to first place in 1991—the first worst-to-first team to make the World Series.[1] And for fourteen consecutive baseball seasons, they won their division—an all-time record for any major professional sports team. They became a symbol not of futility but of consistent excellence. (Considering their history, they needed all fourteen of those years to establish a new image.)

Their on-field attitude over that time makes for an interesting psychological study. In 1991, their late-season surge to win the division was so unexpected that both the team and the city reached unprecedented heights of fervor. At the first pitch of the first home play-off game, the stadium was packed. The headlines the next morning took up half the front page—not the front page of the sports section but of the whole newspaper. Atlanta had pennant fever, and every nuance of every postseason game was approached with sharp focus and intensity. Like gritty but vastly overmatched underdogs in a feel-good movie, they won the National League pennant with impressive skill, a lot of determination, and even more adrenaline.

But as the play-off spectacle became an annual ritual—with only one World Series win to show for it—"Braves frenzy" cooled. *Play-off game* and *sellout* were no longer synonymous. Many fans remained aloof during the play-offs, preferring to wait until the Braves got to the World Series to invest their hearts in the team again. It's hard on a heart to keep getting its hopes up only to be disappointed by another play-off letdown. And it wasn't only the fans. The players' attitudes—even of those who joined the team after those early years of success—stabilized. The team developed that mature quality that comes only from experience and that commentators can't resist pointing out—the calm confidence that doesn't get rattled when you're behind on the scoreboard. The kind of mettle it takes to win championships. Psychological toughness. A businesslike manner. A cool-as-a-cucumber demeanor.

The problem was that whenever the World Series was on the line, no significant surge of adrenaline carried the team. Of course, it *does* help to remain calm in those tense situations; but when calm comes at the price of enthusiasm, it can do more harm than good. Though the players would adamantly deny playing uninspired baseball, their laid-back demeanor clearly hindered them in play-off series after play-off series for years, and they were often defeated by teams that resembled overmatched underdogs in a feel-good movie—the kind of team they themselves once were. Desperate teams with loads of passion beat the team with the more talent and skill. Regularly.

That's how underdogs win championships. No matter how much media analysts laud the even keel of maturity, sentiments side with the long shot. If games were played on paper, the teams with the most talent and skill would always win. But everyone knows they often don't—that's why Vegas oddsmakers are still in business—and there are only two reasons for the anomaly: The "better" team doesn't execute its plays as it did in the past, or it loses the battle of intensity. And usually those two reasons have a lot to do with each other.

It's like that in almost every sport. Two teams can play on the same field, but if there's a passionate home crowd, one of them has a distinct advantage. Theoretically, this should have no real influence on the game. The influence is there nonetheless, however, as standings and bookies alike can testify. No one knows how to plug it into a formula, so analysts just call it an "intangible" when they're predicting the winner. But it feels very tangible. An involved crowd is a blunt instrument of psychological warfare. It can build up the esteem of the home team and destroy the esteem of the visitors. It can swing the tides of momentum and create a climate of victory. And it can do all that without a single member of the crowd ever touching the field, the players, or the ball. Why? Because emotions are contagious, motivating, and very, very powerful.

In modern evangelical thought, level-headed maturity is a very desirable quality. It's a sign of spiritual development, and rightfully so. But sometimes underdog believers can do greater things for God with a spiritual adrenaline rush that comes with radical, passionate devotion. The levelheads look down on that enthusiasm because it seems so immature, but in many ways that's what "the faith of a child," which Jesus commended,[2] should look like. Maturity and momentum rarely come in the same package.

A BATTLE OF EMOTIONS

A young shepherd went to the front lines one day to take his brothers some bread. Rather than finding an army of inspired, energized warriors engaged in the heat of battle, he instead encountered troops who were "dismayed and greatly afraid" (1 Samuel 17:11), day after day enduring enemy taunting without doing anything about it.

Maturity and momentum rarely come in the same package.

While there, he witnessed this mockery from the champion of Gath and weighed his options. He calculated the odds of winning in hand-to-hand combat with this intimidating giant of a man and decided to go for it. Slingshot against spear, cloth against armor, weakness against strength. Yes, this was the logical thing to do.

Not a very inspiring story, is it? It's not completely true, either. David's response was not exactly rational, calculated, and levelheaded.

He was actually very offended by Goliath, appalled by Israel's lack of response, and zealous for the name of the Lord. So he risked his life to defend God's armies against the taunts of an evil enemy. He acted on his feelings and won.

We normally don't encourage people to act on their feelings. We've seen how that can get someone into trouble, and we certainly don't want trouble. We want rational decisions made in the calm of careful reasoning. We commend people with a good head on their shoulders and worry about those with a wild heart. We may love our heroes after the battle, but they're the same people we called fools before. We discourage the Davids of God's Kingdom because they sometimes just don't think straight.

The interplay of facts and emotions in the story of David and Goliath is fascinating. First Samuel 17 begins with a long recitation of dismal facts: The armies are gathered on two mountains with a valley in between; Goliath is an extremely large warrior—six cubits and a span, in case you were wondering; he has elaborate metal armor and weaponry (every part listed by material and weight); and he taunts the Israelites daily. And the result of this list of facts is fear and dismay. An entire army—a very experienced, battle-tested, mature army—is paralyzed by one man.

When David arrives on the scene, however, facts take a back seat to faith. "Have you *seen* this man who has come up?" the soldiers ask, pointing out the circumstances in order to quell the emotions (v. 25, italics added). But to David, it doesn't seem to matter what the giant looks like. "Who is this uncircumcised Philistine, that he should defy the armies of the living God?" (v. 26). It's a rhetorical question, but one can easily imagine the men of Israel reciting the list of facts in response. It wouldn't have made any difference. David, very much in tune with God's heart over the situation, was fueled by a gut reaction to the Philistine's slander of the holy.

David's emotion is met with counteremotions: his brothers' anger at his "presumption" and their suspicion of his motives. Eventually David's words reach the ears of King Saul, and the young shepherd is summoned. His first words to the king are revealing: "Let no man's *heart* fail because of him. Your servant will go and fight with this Philistine" (v. 32, italics added). Again, the facts are repeated to him. "You're too young and inexperienced. He's highly trained and battle tested. He's really, really big." To satisfy unbelieving minds, David pulls out a few stats of his own—past experiences of combat with lions and bears who endangered his flocks. The same Saul who has dismissed David's zeal as unrealistic is now persuaded by the facts of past victories. He decides to let him fight.

When David goes out to face Goliath, the giant sees the facts and is offended. "Am I a dog, that you come to me with sticks?" (v. 43). David is unmoved. In emotionally charged language, he tells Goliath what is about to happen and then gives him the reason: "that all the earth may *know* that there is a God in Israel" (v. 46, italics added). In other words, "You are going to be humiliated, and we are going to celebrate in order to demonstrate the truth of the God of Israel." Circumstances and feelings work together to prove a point. All through this story, one heart goes against many minds in hand-to-hand combat, and the heart wins.

VULCAN CHRISTIANITY

I'm not sure today's brand of discipleship produces many Davids. The human soul includes a mind (intellect), a will (intention to act), and emotions (sentiment). That's not a precise division of the soul because neither God nor biblical writers broke down our personhood into smaller elements.[3] But when we teach people what it means to become Christlike, we generally emphasize the importance of understanding God's Word and the necessity of applying it. We cover the mind and the will. But when we discuss the role of emotions, we minimize their importance. We train people not to act according to feelings because feelings are unreliable. The implicit message in that, of course, is that our understanding and actions *are* reliable—a gross overestimation of human reason, in my opinion. But we trust objectivity and treat subjectivity with great suspicion. And because emotions are so subjective, they fall outside the realm of discipleship.

Everyone I know who preaches and teaches about Christian growth and discipleship acknowledges the validity of emotions. But it's not enough to acknowledge their validity if they are treated as second rate. It's one thing to allow feelings as acceptable but quite another to seek them as purposeful. No matter how much we *say* emotions are important, we still don't *act* as though they really are. When we recognize

> We trust objectivity and treat subjectivity with great suspicion. And because emotions are so subjective, they fall outside the realm of discipleship.

feelings as integral to our God-given personalities yet always try to subject them to our rational processes, the result is a soul that feels trampled on—which can lead to resentment of God and his purposes for our lives. It's not enough to tolerate feelings as normal and natural; we have to actively ask God to cultivate the right ones within us.

The predominant evangelical response to the different aspects of our being is illuminating. When our understanding is out of line with God's Word, what do we teach? Conform it to the image of Christ.

When our actions are out of line with God's Word, what do we teach? Conform them to the image of Christ. And when our emotions are out of line with God's Word, how do we respond? We call them unreliable and ignore them until they go away. We seek to follow Jesus in mind and will, and our feelings had better submit.

The result is what I call "Vulcan Christianity."[4] Perhaps you remember Mr. Spock from the original Star Trek series. He was half-Vulcan, and since Vulcans don't have emotions, he was always able to do the right thing without pesky human sentiment getting in the way. Feelings could never be allowed to interfere with logic. His objective approach to every situation made him a highly valuable crew member. Whatever was expedient or profitable for the most people involved and for the sake of the ultimate goal, that's what he would recommend. He was the ultimate utilitarian.

Evangelical Christianity has long produced half-Vulcan disciples. We're glad when emotions are present, but we don't trust them and we don't do much to conform them to the image of Christ. We adamantly insist that they have no bearing on our decisions. They become appendages to our personalities, not core attributes that need to be synchronized with God's emotions. If we experience the joy of the Father or the peace of the Kingdom, that's great. But it certainly isn't necessary, according to our sermons and curriculum.

Another side of this dynamic is in terms of our actions alone: willpower Christianity. We figure out the right thing to do and then plug away at it until we've developed the right habits. There's certainly a place for spiritual habits and discipline, but if this is our entire approach to the faith, there's absolutely nothing to distinguish our approach from that of the Pharisees of Jesus' day. Theirs was an intellectually deciphered, habitual religion that we call ritualism. It's empty obedience. While we don't practice the same habits that the Pharisees and scribes did, and while we generally try to apply grace more liberally than they did, many of us still depend on their methodology for living the Christian life: Figure out the truth, then make yourself do it as a regular practice. But the kind of spiritual newness and abundance that Jesus promises is qualitatively different.

That absolutely does *not* mean that doing the will of God is unimportant. It's vital. The difference for us is the spirit behind our action. Is it intellectual understanding? Social pressure? Self-discipline? Or is a new heart at the center of our discipleship motivating us and creating new desires within us? The difference is that many Christians act a certain way because that's what Christians are supposed to do, and others act that way because that's who they are in Christ. One is death, the other is life.[5] One tells a brother or sister, "I show love to you because I'm obedient," and the other says, "I show love to you because I actually love you." We all have to fall back on raw obedience in dry times, but that should be the exception. For many Christians, however, raw obedience is the norm.

When our teaching and literature emphasize the importance of obedience while rarely mentioning the importance of *heartfelt* obedience, we've got a horribly imbalanced gospel, just as the religious leaders Jesus confronted had a horribly imbalanced understanding of the law and the nature of God. We give the wrong impression when our presentation of truth implies that (1) application is paramount, (2) understanding is important, and (3) emotions are a nice benefit that we can enjoy while supplies last. Where is the new heart in all of that? Salvation is meant to produce not only a renewed mind[6] but also a new heart,[7] and the new heart is primary. But in our hierarchy of Christian growth, feelings and desires lag far, far behind.

Willpower Christianity or "vulcanism" will drive us to the Cross and drill into us the need to deny ourselves daily—for a while. But eventually it will burn us out. We'll die daily without the corresponding resurrection of Jesus' life within us that we're supposed to have. Christianity without joy—whether taught or actually practiced—is a heavy burden. And while Vulcans may avoid making mistakes, they rarely defeat any giants. They don't make for good underdogs. They win tactical battles, not desperate ones.

However your theology understands the human soul, I believe that the mind, the will, and the emotions are designed by God to act as a coequal trinity—just as they clearly did in Jesus. They are to inform one another, synchronize with one another, and function as a single unit. When they don't, the result is something less than Christlike and therefore falls far short of the glory of God.

Here's how that breaks down specifically. When the will becomes the primary emphasis of discipleship, the result is legalism. We focus on "doing"; we're all action, whether the heart's in it or not. So you don't understand why God commanded something? Doesn't matter; *do it anyway*. Don't feel like it? So what? *Do it anyway*. And while there are occasions when that's exactly the right approach to take, it's a terrible lifestyle. We become obedient to a law without being in a relationship with the Lawgiver. And we know what God thinks about that—or, more accurately, how he *feels* about it. A quick look at the prophets and the ministry of Jesus reveals his disapproval. "Well did Isaiah prophesy of you hypocrites," Jesus said pointedly, "as it is written, 'This people honors me with their lips, but their heart is far from me'" (Mark 7:6).[8] In other words, it really matters to God that our hearts be involved in our obedience. Otherwise, it's not true obedience.

When, on the other hand, the mind becomes the main focus, we get a form of mental Christianity that can either develop into an academic exercise or simply an intellectual assent to the truths of the gospel without an actual acceptance of them. One path gets us tied up in long discussions on religious philosophy and systematic theology—neither of which is bad in itself, though neither is enough to save or to satisfy—and the other fools us into thinking we're living the Christian life when all we're really doing is nodding our heads when the pastor preaches.

After all, even demons, James says, believe in God[9]—and with a clearer understanding than many of us have, I might add. Yet their understanding doesn't accomplish anything. They don't normally obey him, although there are times when God forces them to do what he says, as when Jesus commanded demons to come out of people and they had to respond. But without exception, they don't love him. They have understanding, and they can be forced to comply with God's will. But they can't, and don't, have a deep spiritual connection with God.

It's important to understand the gospel and to know how to defend and teach it, but God wants more than understanding from us. He wants the joys of relationship and a heart connection that goes deeper than the mind and the will.

An overemphasis on emotions is just as imbalanced as a primary focus on the mind or the will, but the warnings against emotionalism are much more familiar to us. So many of them have been issued from Western pulpits and seminaries that most Christians are at least aware that this can be a problem. Our focus on the mind and the will is, in part, a response to what we've seen in purely emotional faith that has little truth or obedience to support it. Some people really do believe God isn't present if they don't actually feel him, and some act solely on their emotions without Scripture or reason guiding them. Emotionalism is, in fact, a dangerous situation, and we're right to warn against it. But in aiming at that enemy so often, we allow other enemies to sneak up on us. We're highly prejudiced against one type of imbalance and alarmingly tolerant of the others.

EMOTIONAL DISCIPLESHIP

The preacher grew more passionate and animated with every word. "It's really important—I can't stress this enough—that you feel the same way that God feels. So much of your discipleship will be determined emotionally. It's the key to the motivation that drives you. If you really want to be Christlike, you need to pay attention to your feelings! You need to carefully cultivate them to be like his."

Have you ever heard that in a sermon? Yeah, me either. I would love to footnote that quote, but I don't know anyone who has ever said it, so it's a total fabrication. Because of our deep suspicion of emotions, we're more accustomed to the following maxims:

"Faith isn't a feeling."

"Love isn't a feeling."

"Worship isn't a feeling."

"Feelings are fickle, so never trust them."

"Mountaintop experiences never last."

"Emotional worship services are superficial."

"Working a congregation up into an emotional frenzy has nothing to do with whether the Spirit is there."

"It's easier to act your way into a feeling than feel your way into an action."

"Do what's right, and the feelings will follow."

"Discipleship based on emotions is a roller-coaster ride."

"When the feelings are gone, your devotion to Christ will be gone."

Every one of these statements is true—in the right context. But ask yourself how well they respect each aspect of a disciple's personality. They elevate the mind and the will by reducing the role of emotions. I used to preach many of these principles, so I'm well aware of how they kept me in discipleship drudgery for years by turning faith into simply a "know it and do it" endeavor.

I've moved to parts of the country I wasn't interested in to do ministry I didn't have a heart for simply because it seemed like a rational, potentially productive, sacrificial thing to do. I've accepted dysfunction in certain unpleasant relationships because I told my heart to shut up and refused to let my God-ordained discontentment speak to me. For years I kept asking the Spirit to fill and empower me but allowed no room for him to work. Anytime some semblance of an emotion came into the picture, I'd resolve not to let it motivate me or, even worse, become the basis of a decision. I didn't want to be "ruled" by emotions. So I kept as many of them as possible at arm's length and ended up pretty depressed. Suppressing or ignoring the heart God put within me has, at times, affected the course of my life just as negatively as being tossed around by my feelings would have. As is often said, truth out of balance is error.

For years I kept asking the Spirit to fill and empower me but allowed no room for him to work. Anytime some semblance of an emotion came into the picture, I'd resolve not to let it motivate me or become the basis of a decision.

I tense up whenever I see an article or hear a sermon decrying emotionalism in the church—which is almost every week. I recently read an article that went into great detail about how completely unrelated worship and feelings are. It didn't say emotions were inappropriate in worship, of course. No one teaches that. The message was that emotions are only secondary. And the answer, this writer said, was to understand worship as a primarily cognitive experience.

I read another article that same week that emphasized how God is our Father, our Teacher, our Lord, our Savior, our Master, and on and on—but when we worship him as our Lover, we've crossed a line of familiarity that we have no business crossing. Worship is to be an act of awe and reverence, the author said. The intimacy of a lover is not appropriate to apply to God.

Do a Web search for the terms *Christian* and *emotions* and you'll see what I mean. When I searched, in a matter of seconds I found an article that called emotionalism a cult, one that said our focus on emotions amounts to self-worship, one insisting that celebration is a spiritual-looking disguise to cover up for disobedience, one explaining how emotions fit with the heresies of mysticism and witchcraft, and so on. All of these writers would agree that there's a proper place for emotions in the spiritual life—in principle. But by speaking so loudly and harshly against feelings, they define emotions' "proper place" so narrowly that few real emotions could actually fit there. God-honoring feelings become a theoretical possibility, not a fulfilling experience.

I don't want to name any of these authors because I respect them and agree with them about a lot of things. But on the issues of emotions, I passionately disagree. It's true that emotions carry many pitfalls with them, but so do doctrinal understanding and practical application. Doctrine invariably defines or describes God in ways that he doesn't describe himself. (Notice that the Bible, while being very theological, is not by any means a systematic theology.) And practical application is invariably reduced to a system of how-to principles that may or may not allow room for the voice of God at a particular moment.

I have a lot of questions that these critics don't really deal with in their arguments. For example, where does Scripture say that our cognitive experiences are better arbiters of truth than our emotional experiences? What about all of those biblical examples of rejoicing, shouting, dancing, weeping, and falling in the presence of the Lord, even when the mind can't grasp what's going on? And if God as "lover" is an inappropriate image for worship, doesn't that kind of undermine the whole "bride of Christ" theme in Scripture? Is it therefore wrong to interpret Song of Songs allegorically as God's love for his people, as many Jewish and Christian theologians have done for centuries? Or to attend that wedding in Revelation 21?

I agree with critics of emotionalism when they argue that the point of Christian worship is not to work oneself into a frenzy. But when they argue that emotions aren't a key aspect of Christian growth or essential to bond with God, I strongly disagree. To every critic who laments the growing emotional flavor of many church movements today and wonders why these Christians are so "experience oriented," I'd like to pose this question: *Why aren't you?* Biblically, one can make a vastly better case for highly emotional, experience-based Christianity than for unemotional, cold-doctrine Christianity. I don't recall anywhere in Scripture where we're commanded to deny the feelings we have. Conform them, yes. Eliminate them, no. In fact, Scripture rarely, if ever, rebukes anyone for being too emotional, while it clearly encourages people to be *more* emotional. "Rejoice and be glad." "Be strong and courageous." "Serve the Lord with gladness." "Shout with joy." If we want to conform to New Testament Christianity more than to our largely secular culture, we'll celebrate the swells of emotion returning to the church.

Those who lament emotional displays in the church would get along well with Michal. Perhaps you remember her. She was David's first wife, the one who was embarrassed by his exuberant dancing as he brought the ark of the covenant into Jerusalem. He was making a fool of himself, she said. A king should never act so undignified, so reckless, so obviously and superficially showy for the people around him. And how did God respond to this wise, cautious, rational approach? He rebuked Michal by making her barren for the rest of her days. We never hear from her again.

That's how God feels—yes, *feels*—about those who are so paranoid of excess that they quench the Spirit. He doesn't like it at all.

It sounds very spiritual to talk about discipleship and worship as rational, cognitive, fact-based, feeling-denying endeavors. That's because many throughout history have excluded emotions, for all practical purposes, from the Christian life. Too many followers of Jesus have reinterpreted "deny yourself and take up your cross" as "suppress your feelings and desires and die." It seems so unselfish and otherworldly—even inhuman—which, if you're trying to escape the human condition, is very appealing.

But that's just an illusion of spirituality. The Gnostics did the same kind of thing and were roundly condemned by the church for departing from orthodox, apostolic teaching.[10] They called the material world corrupt and pursued only ethereal, "spiritual" matters. They believed Jesus only *appeared* to live in a physical body; he died and was raised in spirit only. Like their spirit-teacher, Gnostic Christians were to ignore the flesh and even seek to escape it. In effect, Gnostics denied what God had created in order to attain to a higher plane of life. That's closely related to what nonemotional Christianity tries to do.

THE FIDDLER'S BALANCE

The musical *Fiddler on the Roof* is a great example of this tension between the mind, will, and emotions. Tevye the milkman is busy raising his five daughters according to Jewish traditions in prerevolution Russia. That means that when it's time to find a husband, each daughter is at the mercy of a committee made up of her parents and a matchmaker. But one by one, the oldest three daughters defy this tradition. The eldest, Tzeitel, marries a poor tailor who will not be able to provide her with material comforts. But in her eyes that doesn't matter; they love each other.

Marrying for "love" is a huge break from tradition, and it challenges Tevye's assumptions about relationships. He eventually relents and allows the marriage, but then he has to deal with a second assault on tradition. The next-oldest daughter, Hodel, falls in love with a man who asks her to marry him—after he returns from helping with the revolution in Kiev. Tevye doesn't want his daughter engaged to someone who would abandon her like that. But the couple inform him that they're asking only for his blessing, not his permission. Hodel doesn't just attempt to influence the rules, as the first one did. She circumvents them. Why? Because she's in love.

The third daughter, Chava, pushes the issue even further—too far for Tevye. She wants to marry a Christian. When she elopes with him, Tevye refuses even to talk to her again, much less bless such an ill-conceived marriage. He faces a choice between his faith as he knows it and his daughter as she is, and he chooses his faith. In his mind, it's the right thing to do. Understanding the rules and strictly obeying them finally trump love.

Between Hodel and Chava's romances—a pivotal moment in the plot between a barely acceptable marriage and an unacceptable one—Tevye wrestles with the issue of whether feelings of love should carry the same weight as a time-honored principle. "Do you love me?" he sings to his wife. "Do I *what*?!" she sings back. It has never even crossed her mind, apparently. He asks again, and she considers the irrelevant idea. "For twenty-five years I've washed your clothes, cooked your meals, cleaned your house, given you children, milked the cow; after twenty-five years, why talk about love right now?" He presses the question, and she finally concludes that all of that activity must equal love.[11]

To some degree, and by some definitions, it probably does equal love. But to most of us, it doesn't sound like a very fulfilling marriage. You really have to lower your expectations to be content with a relationship like that.

That's exactly what many Christians have done. Following Jesus has, in many of our lives, turned from being a joyful interaction to a pattern of committed activity. Why? Because feelings aren't "reliable." Though every member of the audience is pulling for love to win out in each daughter's marriage, we Christians would have a completely different perspective if Tevye's sacred traditions were closer to biblical principles. Like him, we'd bristle at the thought of sacrificing our traditions at the altar of a feeling we haven't even mentioned in the first twenty-five years of our own marriage. Tevye is like us, trying to hold on to what he knows to be true while dealing with the emotions swirling around him. It's a high-stakes, relationship-altering contest between principle and passion. And in his mind, principle should win.

There's a reason the audience is relieved and satisfied when love wins out over reason. It isn't that we don't value reason or realize its importance, and we certainly don't want people to be *un*reasonable. But we live in a world that's desperate for wholeness, and the mind isn't going to give it to us. We want our hearts to be fulfilled, our yearnings to be satisfied, our deepest cores to be deeply touched. And when principle and passion butt heads, something inside us wants passion to win.

Why do Cinderellas always get their princes when we're writing the story? Why do we pull so desperately for good and true emotions to come out on top of their rivals like underdogs defeating a perennial champion? Because there's a special connection between the Holy Spirit and the human heart. The things of God are not intelligible to the rational mind and can only be perceived intuitively. Revelation often comes through communion with the Spirit, and the mind has to catch up later and try to figure it all out. This happens in individual situations, such as Mary's news from Gabriel that she will bear a child while still a virgin—"How can this be?" her mind wonders in amazement while her heart accepts the report.[12] It also occurs at a macro level, such as the history of systematic theology, which attempts to translate the experiential truth of the Bible into the language of religious and philosophical principles. If we think we can deduce God's will or his character intellectually, we're going to be tragically disappointed. His ways are not *il*logical, but they'll blow a circuit in our brains if we try to grasp them. They are *extra*logical—above our reasoning—and only the heart can perceive them by faith.

> *Revelation often comes through communion with the Spirit, and the mind has to catch up later and try to figure it all out.*

This is why a brilliant mathematician and scientist like Blaise Pascal could say, even during the rise of rationalism, that "the heart has its reasons that reason does not know." He understood the limitations of the mind and knew that objective thinking could only take us so far. The mind is finite and fallen, and we cannot know the things of God unless the Spirit endows us with the mind of Christ.[13] The heart is finite and fallen too, of course, but it seems much more capable of diving into the depths of the Spirit and soaring into the heights of heaven. Pascal acknowledged that the passions could trick the mind and lead it astray, but he also believed the mind could do the same to our passions. Though he never would have said that spiritual truth is irrational, he argued that human reason isn't enough to arrive at truth. Knowledge of the mind and of the heart are two different kinds of knowledge, and neither, he asserted, should be allowed to rule the other.

HEARTLESS

Deuteronomy 28 is a landmark chapter in the Old Testament. It's the passage where Moses gives God's instructions to Israel about the ramifications of the covenant. If they are careful to do all that the Lord instructs, they will be blessed in a multitude of ways. If they aren't, they will suffer the curses of disobedience.

Sounds pretty simple, doesn't it? Do good, be blessed. Do bad, be cursed. It's all about what you do. Except for one thing: If you read the passage carefully, it shows that even obedience is not enough. In the midst of a list of dire consequences, one line cuts to the core: You shall serve your enemies in hunger and thirst "because you did not serve the LORD your God *with joyfulness and gladness of heart*, because of the abundance of all things" (vv. 47-48, italics added). In other words, obedience without feelings of joy is not a pleasing obedience to the Lord.

God's purpose for us goes deeper than action. Behind our obedience needs to be a heart that loves the Lord. It's great, for example, to have a predetermined budget that includes giving to ministries and to causes that further God's purposes. That's a rational decision that probably grows out of a heart desire to honor God. But over time that budget can become pretty routine, and the giving can become hardly noticeable. It's still obedient to God's plan for our stewardship. But is it heartfelt obedience? Wouldn't God take more pleasure in a heart that's powerfully moved by his generosity or by his compassion toward someone in desperate need?

That's why the greatest commandment must be followed in all of its fullness. "You shall love the LORD your God with all your heart and with all your soul and with all your might" (Deuteronomy 6:5). In Jesus' quote of that commandment, he replaces "might" with "mind."[14] If word order is important, we should notice which aspect of our being comes first: the heart.[15] But all parts of us are to work together. All elements of our soul have fallen, and all are to be redeemed and transformed into the image of Christ.

Vulcan and willpower Christianity are the result of some very valid concerns about emotionalism, but they are just as off base as the situation they target. They can rule out the Spirit's promptings much too easily. They can lead us to accept the rationale of Goliaths and keep us out of unlikely battles. They can prevent us from zealously, passionately, even recklessly pursuing God's heart. And God, who made us in his image for exactly that purpose, grieves.

the infinite heart

how God feels

HE WAS HARD to get to know—detached, aloof, and far too quiet for my taste. But that's just the nature of some, and there's not much you can do about it until they decide to open up.

Over time, that's just what he did, and a whole new person appeared before me. Underneath what I saw as a cold exterior was an extremely warm heart. His once passionless personality suddenly exploded with focus and zeal. Where I had once perceived passivity, I discovered a driving, relentless purpose. And when he loved . . . well, words can't come close to it. He would overflow with passion and burn with jealousy. I was hooked.

If you're like me, your perceptions of God may have initially been skewed. That's because of how he has been misrepresented over the years—positioned high above emotional swells and untouched by ecstasy, grief, and everything in between. But that description, as we have seen, is a figment of theological imaginations and not the way he presents himself in his own words. He has had powerful and deep emotions from eternity past. It's who he is, and nothing will ever change that.

In my experience of God, he wasn't the one who changed. It was me. I grew up in this world with a distorted picture of his nature, as we all did. The character that "transformed" into a warm, emotional being was warm and emotional all along. I just didn't know that. I'd been told at least several thousand times in my younger years that God loved me, so that wasn't the problem. But let's face it: It's easy to misread the Bible, especially to emphasize some parts of it at the expense of others. As a teenager, I wanted to be a serious disciple of Jesus, so I read a lot about denying myself, making hard sacrifices, loving enemies, turning the other cheek to rude people, going the extra mile even when it hurts, and so on. When those very true and important principles aren't balanced with the joy of the Lord and the extravagance of his grace, they start to feel very heavy. God seemed more and more like a hard master. Did he love me? Of course. But only because he had to, just like a good parent does. It took quite a bit of time, even after reading the Bible several times and intellectu-ally acknowledging God's feelings, to begin to actually perceive him as someone I'd enjoy knowing.

Few people can relate to an emotionless person, much less fall in love with one. We generally connect with people when we see them in life situations that bring out their true feelings—neighbors who develop a rapport while surveying damage from the previous night's storm, for example, or a dating relationship that grows deeper through a crisis in the life of one of the partners. But because Christian theology has a hard time explaining the passions of God, many of us never quite connect with him. Never mind that those emotions are clearly vented on nearly every page of Scripture; our speculations about his infinite nature, omniscience, and detailed foreknowledge seem to undermine the very existence of God's emotions. The result is that we unwittingly strip God of lowly, humanlike emotions and then wonder why we find him distant and detached.

But the reason human beings have such emotions to begin with is that we are made in the image of a God who himself has them. They aren't unique to humanity (though I've heard someone argue quite seriously that they are), and they aren't just a product of the Fall. Scripture clearly shows that our feelings of joy, hope, love, anger, jealousy, grief, and more are given to us by a Creator who has those exact same feelings. What happened at the Fall is that emotions were sinfully distorted. We now base them on the wrong values and perceptions and direct them at the wrong targets. Their distortion, not their existence itself, is the problem.

Because Christian theology has a hard time explaining the passions of God, many of us never quite connect with him.

If we believe the representation of God in a Scripture we believe is inspired by his Spirit, we have to also believe that God is subject to the very emotions he breathed into our psyche. Many educated people think that ascribing emotions to God is a way of humanizing a deity we don't understand, thereby bringing him down to our level. Far from unnecessarily humanizing and debasing him, however,

I believe this idea can elevate us—or at least our perception of who we are as image bearers of God. It validates our feelings as God-ordained representations of his personality. Embracing those feelings as highways into his heart can bring us into deeper relationships with him than we've ever known.

So what exactly are those feelings? And how can we know God has them? Well, according to Scripture, he wears them on his sleeve. The pages of the Bible give us quite a few pictures of the range and intensity of his heart.

LOVE, HATE, AND JEALOUSY

"For God so loved the world. . . ." That's where most people's understanding of the gospel begins—with a familiar verse about the love of the Father. Of any of God's emotions, it's probably easiest to find supportive Bible texts for his love. Even many non-Christians are familiar with the pithy "God is love" statements of 1 John.[1] One of our most revered evangelistic presentations of the last half-century begins with "God loves you and has a wonderful plan for your life."[2] One of the first songs kids learn in Sunday school is "Jesus loves me, this I know." Nearly every wedding in Christendom quotes at least some, if not all, of the verses from 1 Corinthians 13—"Love is patient, love is kind. . . ." (NIV). Even Oprah convinced an agnostic audience member on her talk show a few years ago that he really did believe in God—because, as she put it, "You believe in love, don't you? Then you believe in God."

In asserting the emotions of God, love isn't going to require much proof. The only argument it gets within Christianity is whether it's actually an emotion. Plenty of preachers, teachers, and writers have emphasized that love is not a feeling, but that's because they're trying to emphasize (usually in a message about marriage or enemies—or both) that love is constant and unfailing, even on your worst days when you've lost that lovin' feeling. But if you try to talk about love without using any emotional terminology, it sounds very sterile and, to be honest, unloving. Everyone knows that while love may not always be accompanied by warm, fuzzy feelings, it had better be deeply ingrained with compassionate and affectionate sentiments much of the time. Otherwise, who really cares if they have it?

Most genuine forms of love can't be reduced to actions alone. Feelings have to be involved at some level.

It's important to emphasize the emotions of love, because a lot of Christians have the idea that "love is an action." In truth, it's much more than an action. A supervisor, servant, or caretaker can do what's best for someone without having any love whatsoever for that person. People can behave in the interest of others out of commitment to a promise or contract without any love behind their actions at all. Love *involves* actions—it has to translate into practical life if it's real—but most genuine forms of love can't be reduced to that. Feelings have to be involved at some level.

When applied to God, the result of the "love is an action" belief is a relationship with a deity who will do what's best for us even though he wishes he didn't have to. He may love us, but he doesn't *like* us. With that definition of love, we can easily feel like the problem child that the Father has to put up with, though he doesn't really enjoy being with us very much. It's all duty and no pleasure.

That perception of God's love comes from the finest expositors waxing eloquent about the dispassionate virtues of *agape*, the kind of love Greeks held in highest esteem and that the Gospel writers used most often when referring to Jesus' love. It's a rich, beautiful word, but Christians have taken a secondary emphasis of *agape*—its unconditional character—and, through repetition, made it a primary emphasis. It's true that *agape* is unwavering and enduring, even when the feelings of love aren't present. Plus, it's really the only kind of love we can direct toward our enemies, since we don't generally look forward to seeing them. It's unconditional, not subject to whims and moods and adverse circumstances. But in addition to implying willful benevolence, it still also carries heavy connotations of deep affection. Because of our correct but overemphasized lessons in applying the term to difficult commitments, selfless sacrifices, and unlovely enemies, many believers have come to understand *agape* as the kind of love that endures only because it has to. It's effective, but it usually isn't very fun. That's not a great description of God's love, and as a result, we forget the affection God feels for his people.

Agape isn't the only kind of love God feels. For one, we know God experiences *phileo*, the friendship kind of love that includes personal attachment and sentimental feelings. This kind of love is applied to God several times in the New Testament: It's how the Father loves the Son, for example;[3] how the Father loves us because we have loved the Son;[4] and how Jesus loved Lazarus.[5] And when Jesus called his disciples "friends," he was using a word derived from *phileo* because he felt strong affection for them.

The other common Greek word for love is *eros*—romantic and/or sexual love—and we don't see that applied to God anywhere in the New Testament. So why bring it up? Because even though the word isn't used of God, the concept is—quite often, in fact.

The Greek connotations of romantic love overtly included the pagan origin of the word (Eros was the mythological offspring of the goddess Aphrodite) and its overlap with all kinds of ritual and deviant sexuality. So naturally it doesn't exactly make a great descriptor of our holy Creator. But God is surely a romantic, as the abundance of wedding imagery in Scripture testifies. Many rabbinic scholars consider the Sinai covenant[6] an engagement contract and interpret the Song of Songs as an allegory of God's love for his people. The prophets, as we've seen, use the imagery of a forsaken lover to describe God's relationship with Israel. Jesus identified himself as the Bridegroom of his people and performed his first miracle at a wedding celebration. And all of Scripture ends with a wedding between the Son and his bride, the church.

It's only appropriate that we first consider the love of God when discussing his emotions. But contrary to popular opinion, love is not the only attribute of God. We've already mentioned his jealousy, a necessary component of any real love. It's a holy jealousy, to be sure. Some translations of 1 Corinthians 13:4 state that "love is not jealous," but we know that this must be more closely related to selfish envy than to a passion for exclusive love. Our jealousy can be petty, spiteful, and manipulative. God's jealousy, however, only shows up when the people whose hearts he fashioned for himself turn those hearts to things that will ultimately leave them empty. If *agape* love and intolerance for love's rivals were mutually exclusive, God would have contradicting characteristics—which, of course, he doesn't. He experiences very legitimate jealousy. Otherwise, he wouldn't have told us repeatedly in his Word that he is a jealous God, and even that his name is Jealous.[7]

What Does God Hate?

And then there's his hatred. We're so used to hearing that "God is love" that it's hard for us to imagine his hatred; but it's there. It only makes sense, too. Think about it: If you love someone dearly, don't you tend to hate the things that threaten or harm that person? It isn't that God is filled with hate for the sake of hatred. His loving nature demands that he hate whatever contradicts or opposes his love.

Here's a sampling of God's hatreds:

• *Idolatry.* He abhors it as much as a loving husband would hate the open prostitution of his wife. Toward her personally, he's jealous. Toward the objects of her sin, he burns with hatred. Idolatry is essentially a choice to love and worship something other than God, and whatever the object of that love is, it's far less worthy than he is. This is not only spiritual adultery; it's the equivalent of sleeping with an abusive, filthy lover because the charming, righteous, affectionate zillionaire just doesn't satisfy you. That, according to God, is worth hating. It interferes with his love most unreasonably. Two clear statements of his hatred of idolatry are Deuteronomy 12:31 and 16:22, but there are many more. When God speaks of things he detests ("abominations," in many versions), idolatry is at the top of the list.

• *Pride.* It was Satan's downfall.[8] Proverbs 8:13 explicitly says that God hates pride, but his revulsion to it is clear throughout Scripture. God opposes the proud and gives grace to the humble,[9] and the prophets bring up that fact repeatedly. Anytime we see pride rear its ugly head in the Bible (and in our own lives), destruction—or at least a very humbling experience—is sure to follow.

• *Violence.* "His soul hates the wicked and the one who loves violence" (Psalm 11:5). Cruelty and bloodshed are blatant contradictions to God's character and destroy his most beautiful creations. Imagine longing for a child for years and then having that desire fulfilled. Then while holding that precious, beautiful baby in your arms, someone comes along and stabs her with a knife. What emotions would you have? That's how God feels about the attempted mutilation of his children. Anything less than hatred would be unloving and irrational.

• *Sexual sins.* The intimate union between husband and wife is a picture of God and his people[10] and Christ and his church.[11] Because it is such a powerful image of God's heart, the enemy and sinful flesh have conspired to come up with myriad ways to twist, distort, counterfeit, and otherwise corrupt this aspect of the image of God. God's sexual standards are not given to us to prevent us from enjoying life, but to lead us to true enjoyment in representing his heart for his people. That's why every deviancy in Scripture is "an abomination" to the Lord.[12] It vandalizes a sacred masterpiece.

• *Deception.* Our Father is "the God of truth."[13] Satan, however, is a deceiver. "When he lies, he speaks out of his own character, for he is a liar and the father of lies" (John 8:44). Deception takes what is true and right and twists it around to create false impressions. When we do that to each other, it's tragic. When Satan does that to God, it's devastating. (You may recall, for example, the results of that debacle back in Eden.) So any hint of deception, whether in financial matters, personal relationships, competitive positions, or any other area of life, is an affront to the God of perfect integrity.[14] Proverbs 12:22 reads, "Lying lips are an abomination to the LORD, but those who act faithfully are his delight."

- *Scheming.* The Lord hates "a heart that devises wicked plans" (Proverbs 6:18). God knows the plans he has for us, plans for good and not for evil.[15] So it only makes sense that plans based on deception and manipulation would violate his purposes and anger him. Wouldn't it bother you if someone diverted a child of yours from the blessing you intended to give? Or got him tangled up in a set of circumstances nearly impossible to get out of? That's how God feels about manipulative scheming. It's messing with a member of the royal household, and there will be repercussions.

- *Slander.* Having been a victim of very public slander more times than any of us can count, God loathes it. His character has been impugned constantly from the first deception in the Garden until now, and many people have no idea who he is because of it. Not only does it offend him for his own name's sake, he's offended for our sake when it happens to us. He doesn't enjoy his children wearing inaccurate labels any more than we do. The Lord hates "a false witness who breathes out lies" (Proverbs 6:19). He will not endure those who slander in secret.[16]

- *Contentiousness.* The three persons of God are in perfect unity, and Jesus prayed that that's exactly the kind of unity his followers would experience.[17] The Lord therefore hates the "one who sows discord among brothers" (Proverbs 6:19). It's essentially an attack on the fellowship of the Trinity among his people. Those who stir up dissension in Scripture are always defeated in the end.

- *Robbery.* "I hate robbery," God says (Isaiah 61:8). That's pretty straightforward. The merciful Father, who is full of compassion and grace, giving all things freely to those who love and believe him, is opposed to those who take his blessings from those to whom he gave them. Imagine your child crying her eyes out because someone took the Christmas gift you gave her. That picture explains why God hates stealing.

- *Complaining and arguing.* God takes complaining personally. He made that clear on numerous occasions in the wilderness, when his recently delivered people started whining about his lack of provision. On every occasion he got angry, one time hurling fire on the outskirts of their camp,[18] and letting a generation die in the desert for their pessimism.[19] "My heritage . . . has lifted up her voice against me," the prophet Jeremiah heard him say. "Therefore I hate her" (Jeremiah 12:8).

- *Superficial, insincere worship.* Jesus felt compelled to remind Israel's leaders of a well-known passage from Isaiah: "This people honors me with their lips, but their heart is far from me" (Mark 7:6, quoting Isaiah 29:13). In fact, most of the prophets pointed out this detestable condition. False or superficial worship undermines the very reason we were created—to glorify God. When devotional practices become empty rituals, they are revolting to God.[20]

- *Injustice.* The Lord is a God of justice.[21] Therefore, he violently opposes injustice.[22] In fact, according to Ezekiel, the greatest sin of Sodom was not its sexual immorality (though that was great), but its lack of compassion toward the destitute. "This was the sin of your sister Sodom: She and her daughters were arrogant, overfed and unconcerned; they did not help the poor and needy" (Ezekiel

16:49, NIV). God's heart is always with the poor, the downtrodden, the oppressed, the widows, and the orphans. He frequently expresses his hatred and anger over the causes of such conditions.

- *Divorce.* Nearly every Christian is familiar with God's hatred for divorce because it's the hatred we most often cite.[23] I heard a preacher say one time that the sin of divorce is unique because it's the only sin God singles out as one that he hates. Well, no. Read the Bible. We've unfairly portrayed people who are divorced as the worst of sinners while ignoring many of our more flagrant but secret sins of the heart, probably because divorce is an easy target. God hates all sin, and all of us have done something that God hates. (Refer to the above list if you have trouble thinking of an example.) But God *does* hate divorce, among other tragedies, and it's for the same reason he hates the sexual sins listed in Leviticus and Deuteronomy. It mars the human illustration of his love for his people. It distorts the picture of our relationship with God.

This list isn't exhaustive, but it's pretty representative. God hates things that conflict with his character, his Kingdom, and his love. In Scripture, his passions run very deep. He hates everything on this list as well as rebellion, witchcraft, divination, and many more contradictions to his Kingdom. If something distracts from, distorts, or demeans his love or his beloved, it's detestable. As we grow to be like him, we will begin to hate those things too.

JOY, GRIEF, AND ANGER

Once we understand what God loves and hates, the rest of his emotions become somewhat self-explanatory. On the positive side, his joy, zeal, and delight are all products of his love. Like us, he will be zealous about fulfilling his love, rejoice every time that fulfillment is advanced, and delight in the objects of his love. On the negative side, his grief and anger are both products of his hatred. Like us, he will be angry at whatever threatens his beloved and grieve every time someone misses his love.

We'll find confirmation of this pattern when we look at what the Bible specifically says about these emotions. Though skeptics question God's wrath, it's really an emblem of his love. If he didn't care, he wouldn't have it. If he didn't have it, his love would be the impotent kind that doesn't get upset even when it's abused and rejected. When God's generosity is taken for granted, when his will is opposed, when his love is undermined by lies, when people oppress the innocent or practice divination or worship false gods, it makes him angry. His wrath is controlled, of course, and he says often that he's slow to anger.[24] He doesn't fly into a rage, act capriciously, or apply his anger unpredictably. But he certainly has it. Regardless of whether we understand it, it's so pervasive in Scripture—especially in the prophets—that arguing against its existence undermines the Bible itself, the same revelation through which we know God exists in the first place.[25] Watering it down may seem like an argument in favor of his compassion, but it actually weakens our understanding of his love. His anger always correlates with his love. Wrath is his response to witnessing something he hates, and hatred is his response to violations of his love. They're all interrelated.

His grief, too, is a by-product of his love. Frequently in the Bible, especially in the prophets, God grieved over the sin and lostness of his people. Jesus wept over Jerusalem,[26] and Paul pointed out that the Spirit can be grieved.[27]

In both positive and negative feelings, God is zealous—fervent and passionate. Though he is thorough in everything he does, he does some things with additional vigor: preserving Judah's remnant,[28] battling for his people,[29] accomplishing righteousness and salvation,[30] and expressing his wrath.[31] When Jesus cleansed the temple by overthrowing the tables of the money changers, he fulfilled a prophecy by demonstrating zeal for his Father's house.[32]

Occasions of his joy also repeatedly revolve around the people he loves and the purposes he pursues for them. One of the most dramatic instances is in Jesus' story of the prodigal son. A father's grief was turned to joy when he saw his repentant son coming from a distance. The father threw a party and joyfully lavished his blessings on the boy, welcoming him back into the family with symbols of the highest honor and inviting everybody within earshot to celebrate. This, Jesus said, is how God feels when people come to him.

God's delight over his people is a consistent theme throughout Scripture, except when his people are rebellious and adulterous, in which case delight turns to grief. But under normal circumstances, those who belong to God delight him. Zechariah 2:8, among other verses, calls Israel "the apple of his eye." Psalm 149:4 says he "takes pleasure in his people." One of the most heartwarming pictures of God in the Bible is at the end of Zephaniah. After explaining how the whole world will be consumed by God's jealous anger,[33] the prophet offers the ultimate comfort in describing what God has promised: "He will take great delight in you, he will quiet you with his love, he will rejoice over you with singing" (Zephaniah 3:17, NIV). The picture is of a father holding a small child and singing lullabies with a huge smile on his face. That's how God represents his feelings for the people he has redeemed.

God also takes great pleasure in his plans and purposes. It was (and still is) his pleasure to hide things from the wise and learned and reveal them to little children—a statement that flowed out of Jesus' mouth when he was, not just coincidentally, "full of joy through the Holy Spirit" (Luke 10:21, NIV). The psalmist certainly expects God to "rejoice in his works" (104:31). David credited his deliverance to God's delight

God's delight over his people is a consistent theme throughout Scripture.

in him,[34] and the queen of Sheba was certain that God delighted in Solomon because of all the blessings he had been given.[35] Psalm 147:11 tells us that he "delights in those who fear him, who put their hope in his unfailing love" (NIV). He also delights in the humble[36] and in those who tell the truth.[37] And when God delights in a man's way, "he makes his steps firm" (Psalm 37:23, NIV).

Not only does God delight in the people he loves, he also delights in himself. He loves his own attributes.[38] In us, that would be arrogance, but with God it's realism. There's nothing greater or higher to take pleasure in than his glory, so both we and he are right to do so.

All of this delighting and rejoicing, of course, doesn't fit with many people's perceptions of God. To many he's a hard master insisting on maximum labor for minimum reward, or a cosmic cop who's stingy with blessings and liberal with punishment. God's joy is one of those unexpected, counterintuitive attributes that we have a hard time picturing, partly because of our own misperceptions and partly because of the multitude of slanderous, treasonous accusations against him that the enemy has sown in this world. But recognizing the truth that God is joyful, that his love causes him to delight in doing good, and that he receives pleasure from those who love and believe him, is a biblical imperative. We're commanded to let that sink in. God is, more often than not, in a really good mood.

MAXIMUM INTENSITY

As we've seen, Scripture is clear about which emotions God has. However, it's quite another thing to understand the intensity of his emotions. We can compare types of feelings with our own, but we have no frame of reference for the brightness with which his feelings burn. They are necessarily more fiery and powerful than anything we can imagine. He is, after all, infinite.

The Bible often uses extreme terms to describe his feelings, especially his negative ones. He has "fierce anger" (Numbers 25:4), "burning anger" (Numbers 32:14, NASB), and "hot displeasure" (Deuteronomy 9:19). He says he is "very jealous for Zion . . . burning with jealousy for her" (Zechariah 8:2, NIV). These are not exaggerations. If anything, they are understatements. His feelings—both positive and negative—are more relentless than ours, infinitely higher and lower than ours, and more intense than any laser beam the world's best scientists can dream of. His feelings can cut through any circumstance and pierce even our own hearts. In fact, he has to hold back not to slay us with either his love or his anger. They're too powerful to unleash on mere mortals except in small doses, and even then they can overwhelm us. When God feels, he feels with enough force to move the universe.

I believe that's one of the reasons God hid Moses in the cleft of the rock and covered his eyes before passing by him. Moses had asked to see God's glory, but the words God used to describe his glory were largely emotion-laden: compassionate, gracious, slow to anger, abounding in love and faithfulness.[39] These words are part of his name,[40] and they would have destroyed Moses with their power.[41] When we say "if looks could kill . . . ," we forget that with God they actually can.

What does this mean for us? First, we need to realize that when we talk about any attribute of God, it's impossible to exaggerate it. All of those times we say or think "yeah, but . . ." to the idea that God loves us, delights in us, rejoices over us, hates sin, grieves over our losses, and is angered by the corruption of his creation and his people, we're making a ridiculous understatement. Whenever an emotion of God—or any aspect of his character—comes to our attention, we'd be on the right track to go ahead and multiply it by a thousand and try to let our minds catch up with the thought. Though our natural tendency is to downplay or rationalize God's revealed feelings in Scripture, we're wrong. We need to push our minds in the other direction.

More than that, however, we need to let his emotions saturate us by thinking about them, asking him to impart them to us, cultivating the moments when we experience them, and finding ways to apply them to other people in our lives. This can be a rather intuitive, ethereal process, but it's nevertheless very real. For example, I spent a week in college trying to imagine I had created every single person I came into contact with. That may initially sound prideful, but I was under no illusion that I had actually made anyone. I just wanted to know how God might feel about them. During the course of the week, I began to feel love for people I had once disliked, patience for people I had once criticized, and compassion for people whom I felt might be going through trials I couldn't see. Instead of being put off by offensive people, I began to grieve over how they were harming themselves spiritually and relationally. It was a very emotionally transforming experience, and I still can't explain it in cognitive terms. That's because our minds and our determination are never going to be able to tap into the heart of God and grasp the way he feels. Only the emotional side of our personalities can do that.

THE FEELINGS GOD NEVER HAS

Many of our feelings don't connect us with God because God doesn't have them. I group these emotions into three main categories:

- *Despair and all of its corollaries*: depression, discouragement, apathy, and hopelessness. God doesn't feel any of these things because he knows the end of every story and he has promised that his purposes will be fulfilled. His love *will* be satisfied.

- *Fear and all of its corollaries*: anxiety, worry, stress, and terror. God is not afraid of anything because all power is his. Nothing can thwart his plans and no one can threaten his security.

- *Bitterness and all of its corollaries*: resentment, hardheartedness, and cynicism. These feelings result from our inability to deal with anger and offenses, as well as our inability to see the big picture and embrace redemption. God doesn't have those inabilities. He doesn't have *any* inabilities. He is victimized by no one, and he has no need to hold on to anger once he has expressed it.

When we encounter these emotions in ourselves, we can be sure that our hearts are not aligned with God's. That doesn't mean we need to kick ourselves in self-condemnation, but it does mean we need to repent in the sense of changing our minds and perspectives. Depression, bitterness, and fear always arise out of misperceptions—our unreliable reason playing tricks on us—and are usually an accurate barometer of our spiritual heartbeats.[42] We can be confident that it is not God's will for us to have these feelings because they aren't consistent with his heart, and his purpose is to conform us to his image. Therefore, these emotions are misplaced. They're perfectly natural, in our fallenness, but they aren't part of the climate of heaven. We need to get rid of them.

God will help with that. One of the greatest prayers you'll ever pray in your life is to ask him for his heart, and when you find true emotions burning within you to the degree you think you just might die, you'll know he has answered. Finite bodies have a hard time coping with the stress of a heart rooted in eternity, but the power that results is life changing. Deep, God-given compassion for "China's millions" is what drove Hudson Taylor to his history-changing mission work. A broken heart for India's orphans and child prostitutes moved Amy Carmichael to rescue thousands of lives from spiritual and physical deprivation. Emotional promptings of the Spirit have led to repentance, mended relationships, outreach to underserved populations, and much more, all because people asked to have God's heart. Fruitful ministries have been born from such prayers, and relationships with God have grown deeper than ever before.

It's God's will for us to conform to his emotions. We are told, "Hate evil, and love good,"[43] just as God hates evil and loves good. We're also instructed to rejoice in his presence, to be thankful, to celebrate with praise and shouting and music, to worship him with gladness, and to detest idols. For people who are used to a two-step discipleship plan—understanding and doing—that's a lot of emotional instruction. But the payoff is worth it. Emotional transformation can bring us into a kind of fellowship with God that we may never have dreamed of. It can give us a sense of fulfillment about our faith and work, and it can bear the fruit of his Kingdom. And best of all, it pleases his heart.

CHAPTER 4

discipleship's missing ingredient
how we connect with God

THEY GATHERED IN Jerusalem to celebrate Pentecost and wait for the power Jesus promised. When it happened—when the Spirit fell on these hopeful believers with many tangible side effects—they experienced a sense of euphoria. "Everyone kept feeling a sense of awe," Luke wrote, adding that they ate meals together "with gladness and sincerity of heart" (Acts 2:43, 46, NASB). That spirit of "one heart and soul" (4:32, NASB) continued for a season, and believers and observers alike were filled with amazement. It was truly a mountaintop experience. [1]

But mountaintop experiences don't last, do they? The emotions eventually die down, and then you're left with the daily grind and the hard life of discipleship. Plugging away, day after day, you try to forget what lies behind and press on with determination, because those feelings just won't linger.

Oops. Wait a minute. That's modern revisionism taking over a biblical story and inserting our own worldview into it. Upon further consideration, let me rewrite that last paragraph:

That highly emotional experience of Pentecost became a lifelong anchor for most of the people who were there. Some of them went to extravagant lengths to share the message with others, even decades later. Many endured extreme persecution because that experience had shaped them irrevocably. Others even died as martyrs with the testimony of the power of that day on their lips. The Kingdom mission never succumbed to trials and temptations because the comfort and presence of the Spirit lasted long beyond Pentecost.

And that day is still fueling our fires two thousand years later. Some of us get pretty excited when we read about it, and we recapture those emotions from time to time when we think of the reality of God being with us. Why not consider pursuing them as a key to our Christian maturity? Just because we experience good feelings doesn't mean those feelings are self-centered. Maybe they can actually point to God and bring him glory.

Paul had a mountaintop experience that glorified the Lord. He was on the way to Damascus to punish some Christians by death or imprisonment, and he had a God encounter. It must have been very traumatic—a tangled mixture of fear, awe, guilt, and amazement. It was very experiential; he didn't encounter this Christ in the pages of Scripture. Not yet. This was personal—objective truth, obviously, but very subjectively revealed—and Paul took the total experience of this encounter with him wherever he went, both the feelings and the facts. He enthusiastically referred to it again and again throughout his ministry because this particular mountaintop experience was a valid, life-changing event. And, apparently, it lasted.

Those are two examples among many of highly charged emotional experiences that changed people's lives and directly affected the course of their ministries. The feelings themselves may not have lasted; it's hard (and unrealistic) to sustain emotional intensity over long periods of time. But the spiritual growth of those moments and the decisions that were made in them certainly had a lasting impact. That's evident in the life of Moses, who had many mountaintop experiences: one at a burning bush and several actually on mountaintops. Each time, a holy transaction took place. He was affected by objective truth but moved by subjective experience. (In fact, when many rational people in the wilderness later questioned Moses' subjective experience, God got very, very angry.[2]) Moses' mind, will, and emotions were all impacted.

The same could be said of Isaiah when he saw the Lord in the temple and cried out, "Woe is me!" and later, "Here am I. Send me."[3] Or of Daniel and his visions.[4] Or of the fear, grief, or apathy that often gripped Israel as a nation and hindered its calling. Nearly every time God acts in Scripture, emotions are associated with the event—not just as an afterthought but as a guiding, empowering agent. The feelings associated with biblical mountaintop experiences had the power to affect the understanding of God's people and influence their actions. And they usually lasted a lifetime.

It's worth noting that when Israel was ready to cross the Jordan and enter the Promised Land, God's message to Joshua, and then Joshua's word to the people, was nothing like an informational meeting.

Neither Joshua nor Israel were told that their feelings didn't matter, that they were to follow what they knew to be true regardless of their inner discomfort. That would have been *true* advice on some occasions, but it wouldn't have been *good* advice here. Instead, they were told again and again to be strong and courageous, not to fear, to be bold, to take heart. Why? Because they were about to do battle. They were about to come up against those "giants" their spies had once been afraid of—well-armed giants guarding huge city walls. This was not time to rationalize. They needed to put their game faces on.

We do too. Whether we're in a battle or simply offering our petitions to the Lord or helping a neighbor, emotional engagement is an important part of our activity. God does not make dispassionate disciples, neither in Scripture nor in any experience I've ever observed. In fact, you can make a pretty good case from the Bible that discipleship *must* involve some strong feelings and even an occasional mountaintop event. God is intensely emotional, and we're designed to relate to him. Therefore, we need to be intensely emotional. Feelings are a vital key to knowing who he is.

A TIN MAN'S TRAVAILS

"I could be kind of human, if I only had a heart."[5] Those words were once sung by a tin man on a yellow brick road, but they could just as easily be sung by many Christians today. The religious instinct in us thinks we need to become devoid of personal preferences in order to be truly spiritual—kind of like the "empty kettle" the tin man felt he was. Little did he know that his empty-vessel condition would become a highly regarded commodity in much of modern Christendom.

Think that's an exaggeration? Consider how many times you've heard a message on emptying yourself and being filled with the Spirit of God. It's a great biblical principle, depending on how you define *empty*, but it translates badly. Many believers hear in that lesson a command to get rid of everything that's in them, so they set about deconstructing the image of God that their Creator intended for them to carry. You have a desire to do something? Remember, for a Christian it's always "not my will but thine." You find pleasure in something that doesn't appear to directly impact the Kingdom of God? Live sacrificially; you're a steward of the gifts God has given you. You're stirred by an emotion? Take up your cross and die daily. Your emotions will lead you astray.

God does not make dispassionate disciples. In fact, you can make a pretty good case from the Bible that discipleship must involve some strong feelings.

Maybe that's an overstatement, but the fact is that many people, myself included, have tried to get rid of certain desires and feelings in the name of denying self, not realizing that those desires and feelings were placed in us by God as a means to pull us in a certain direction or share his heart with us. I've gone to schools and moved to cities that seemed most logical or appropriate for service when my heart was really in other places, all in an effort to deny self. I have a friend who went to seminary because he felt obligated to be "in ministry"—even though his real desire was to make a spiritual impact in the corporate world, an arena where God eventually used him powerfully. History is full of people who chose a marriage partner for practicality rather than for genuine love because "the heart can lead astray." The result of denying God-given desires is almost always less fruitfulness for the Lord and less fulfillment for the individual, with ample regrets mixed in. When we deny *everything* in us, we're denying more than self. We're denying the Spirit who is at work in us both "to will and to work for his good pleasure" (Philippians 2:13). Because we haven't learned to discern the difference between the self and the Spirit, we throw them out together. The result is perpetual emptiness and prolonged discouragement that God seems so distant.

The result of denying God-given desires is almost always less fruitfulness for the Lord and less fulfillment for the individual, with ample regrets mixed in.

Like the tin man, we want to be tender and gentle. And we could, if we only had a heart. But somewhere along the way, someone convinced us that we should be suspicious of our feelings—that the flesh is emotional and the spirit is constant and reliable. So in order to be spiritual, we do whatever we can to suppress our feelings and rely on God, not realizing that the feelings may have actually come from his Spirit.[6]

What we really need to be occupied with as we grow into the likeness of Jesus is not denying human emotions, but having the right ones at the right times to the right degree. We could do that much more easily if we really understood how God feels.

Our religious instincts not only convince us that the emotional flesh wars against the redeemed spirit in us; they convince us that peace, love, and joy belong to God, while anger, hatred, and grief belong to the devil. God's emotions are the happy ones, and Satan's are the negative ones. So we condemn all of our negative feelings as an intrusion into our spiritual growth.

But that's not how the Bible assigns emotions, is it? We've already seen that God has the capacity for hatred, anger, grief, and jealousy.

Our job is not to get rid of all negative emotions, but to get rid of all *misdirected* negative emotions. In other words, it's perfectly acceptable—even required—to hate the things God hates, to be angry about whatever makes him angry, to grieve when he grieves, and to be jealous for the love of his people. We're *supposed* to have an emotional connection with him. Our feelings are supposed to merge with his.

Think about the people you have an emotional connection with. How many of them became close to you through a constant, mutual denial of difficult feelings? How many of those relationships are based on an objective agreement rather than on shared emotional responses? How close do you get to someone when you feel differently on most issues? Or when one of you is intensely interested in an issue and the other is apathetic toward it? In other words, what person close to you is not primarily close *emotionally*?

It's impossible to have any sort of intimacy with someone without an emotional connection. You may share information and understanding with a conversation partner, but unless both of you feel the same way about the information, you don't bond. You may work on a project with a colleague, involved in the same activity day in and day out, but unless you have the same interest and passion invested in that project, you don't bond. Emotions are the glue that cements relationships and makes them worthwhile. Though that flies in the face of most Christian marriage advice, it's true. The fact of your commitment may keep you together in the hard times, but only feelings can draw you closer.

DISCIPLESHIP'S MISSING LINK

I believe this is the key ingredient that's missing from most people's relationship with God. There's a reason we so often wonder why God

63

is distant, why our prayers seem to be bouncing off the ceiling, why we feel so empty when Jesus clearly promised an abundant life. We were designed to throb with the heartbeat of God, but we keep worrying about whether a pulse is even appropriate. Discerning the difference between his heart and ours is too difficult, so we suppress whatever heart is in us. And that's anything but an abundant life.

What's the solution? Embrace the emotions of God. Learn to feel as he feels. Liberate yourself from the kind of theology that tells you your feelings aren't as relevant as understanding truth and practically applying it. Don't make the mistake of elevating feelings above these other aspects of your discipleship, but don't underestimate their importance either. If you want to commune with your God, you not only have to have emotions, you have to emphasize them substantially in your growth.

We were designed to throb with the heartbeat of God, but we keep worrying about whether a pulse is even appropriate.

The best way to do that is to become very attentive to what you feel and why you feel it. When you have a critical attitude toward another person, for example, ask yourself why. Has this person sinned against you? Or do you just not like the way he or she does things? Do you think this person is arrogant because deep down you've noticed a similar attitude in yourself? Are you envious? Or are you unsettled because a Kingdom principle is really at stake and God is prompting you to pray or intervene? Separating the godly feelings from the distorted human ones is the first step in feeling like God.

But that first step is the diagnosis, not the cure. You won't develop a generous heart while focusing on the need to get rid of a critical spirit. The Bible never tells us to get rid of the flesh so we can start living by the Spirit. It's the other way around: "Live by the Spirit, and you will not gratify the desires of the sinful nature" (Galatians 5:16, NIV). When intimate communion with God's Spirit is our focus, the emotional fruit grows and the misplaced sentiments get crowded out. There's no room for them any more.

That's ultimately the solution: a God-saturated heart. This is why so many of our battles come in the form of intimidating circumstances, often through our anxious analyzing and assessments. The enemy doesn't want us to have God's heart, because the last thing he wants is a race of zealous, Kingdom-oriented, Spirit-filled people. God lets him arrange mind-stressing situations for us because that's the soil where his heart can grow in people who lost touch with it long ago. How we feel is extremely important to both God and his enemies. That's one reason discouragement and anxiety are such pesky afflictions among Christians—we have help getting depressed, you know—and it's also one reason the Bible is so big on joy and celebration. Much of it—especially the psalms—is a field manual in how to move emotionally from point A to point B and, ultimately, to feel like God feels.

If this emphasis on feelings were not important, God would describe himself only as our Creator and King. But he's so much more expressive than that. He's our gentle but firm Father, a friend to the followers of his Son, a careful gardener, a compassionate physician, and a zealous Bridegroom anticipating the consummation of his love. It's absolutely inconceivable that emotions would take a backseat in the economy of a God who describes himself this way.

Biblical heroes often acted on an emotion. Take Phinehas, for example. We don't talk about him much today because he isn't politically correct—and, frankly, if we behaved as he did we'd be doing twenty-to-life in a very unpleasant place. In the wilderness before God's people entered the Promised Land, Israel's men were being successfully enticed by foreign women. That's bad enough, but the worst part was that these women often seduced the men to worship their foreign gods. As we've discussed, God hates idolatry. In order to turn "the fierce anger of the Lord" from destroying the people—his anger had already begun to spread a plague through the camps—some of the transgressors were publicly executed by hanging.

While the congregation was still gathered and the people were weeping over this tragedy, an Israelite man brought a Midianite woman into the camp, flaunted his "indiscretion" in plain view of Moses and the congregation, took her into his tent, and began doing what the hanged men had just been punished for doing. Phinehas, a member of the priestly family, was enraged. He got up, found a spear, walked into the bedroom where this couple was coupling, and drove the spear through the man's back, through the woman's belly, and into the ground. They literally died in their sin.

That's a pretty harsh reaction, and most of us today would not condone that sort of vigilante spirituality in our congregations. I'm pretty sure the local police would frown on it too. But God didn't seem bothered by it—not for that time, that purpose, and what that sinful act represented in terms of rebellion and idolatry. In fact, God commended Phinehas for sharing his jealousy for his people.[7] Apparently, Phinehas's feelings lined up with God's.

This is why we can't say that jealousy and anger are wrong. It's fair to point out that sin and selfishness usually aim them in the wrong direction or magnify them beyond reasonable proportions, but we can't say they violate the heart of God. Obviously, according to Scripture, they don't. The solution to negative feelings like those is not to get rid of them but to apply them to the right issues at the right times. They fit into our discipleship if we let God transform them into the righteous anger and jealousy he feels on a regular basis. In the case of emotions God doesn't have, like worry, fear, and despair, the key is to affirm the legitimacy of the unsettled feelings that cause them. God gives us an emotional alarm system that clues us in to situations that aren't quite right. The problem is that our minds filter that alarm through a series of misperceptions, misguided assumptions, and false projections that can result in extreme distress. If we let our minds run wild, the result is often emotional torment. But if we let the alarm simply serve as a call to action—at least prayer, if not more—then it fits well with the feelings of God.

THE PRINCIPLE OF SYNCHRONIZATION

Christiaan Huygens discovered a strange phenomenon in 1665. The Dutch scientist, who had invented the pendulum clock, found himself in a room staring at two of them side by side. He had made both of them at different times, yet he noticed an unexpected coincidence: The pendulums were swinging in exactly the same rhythm.

He checked them repeatedly over a few hours to see if their synchronization exhibited any variation at all. It didn't. Even when he deliberately started them on separate beats, within an hour they would be swinging in unison. And it didn't seem to matter how many clocks were placed in the room; whether two or twenty, they all ended up on the same beat. It was clearly beyond coincidence. Somehow these nonliving objects were influencing each other.

Since then, scientists have been able to identify this principle of "entrainment" throughout the natural world, especially in living creatures. Fireflies in southeast Asia, for example, will light up simultaneously, thousands at a time, with no advance cue from a leader. When several are separated from larger groups and placed in another environment, they begin lighting up in different rhythms, but before long, they're perfectly in sync. And there's more: Women who move into the same household tend, over time, to develop synchronized menstrual cycles. Sperm cells somehow swing their tails in unison as they swim toward an egg. More than ten thousand cells in your heart are independent pacemakers that tell the rest of the heart when to beat—and, like the fireflies, every cell is capable of marching to its own drumbeat. But they don't do that. They influence each other and synchronize, just like "coupled oscillators" everywhere.[8]

I remember reading somewhere that two hearts placed in jars next to each other will eventually develop the same pulse. I'm not sure how that works—how hearts in a jar continue to beat, and why two such jars would ever have occasion to sit next to each other—but the picture fits this principle of entrainment and illustrates a great spiritual truth: Hearts that are close in proximity feed off of each other's rhythm. They learn to beat the same way at the same time.

We see that dynamic in our personal relationships with other people. When you spend a lot of time with someone, you begin to resonate with that person. Your concerns and interests draw closer together, and, in the case of siblings or marriage partners, you often think in the same patterns. Where a real connection has been maintained, what's important to one becomes important to the other. You frequently know how the other feels about a given issue without even asking, because you already know that they feel the same way you feel. Even when your feelings aren't identical, there's a strong empathy for the other's sentiments. Your hearts have developed the same rhythm.

It seems to me that this dynamic ought to apply to our relationship with God too. If the Creator has emotions and made human beings in his image with similar emotions, and if he calls us into relationship with him on nearly every page of Scripture—culminating with a very intimate ceremony at the end of history—our time spent with him ought to transform the way our hearts beat. His loves, delights, and joys ought to rub off on us, along with his anger, displeasure, and grief. At some point in the relationship, we ought to be able to know how he feels without even asking because that's how we feel too. In fact, it makes sense that this melding of hearts is a better definition of discipleship than learning and doing, because neither of those aspects prompts a change in the rest of the soul. Emotional bonds, however, prompt a change in our whole beings. It's the one attribute of our personalities that can synchronize the others.

I don't know how you feel about that, but it encourages me and opens up a whole world of possibilities. My desire to learn about God and to follow his will suddenly thrives in a warm, personal climate. Instead of being pushed upstream in the hard work of spiritual discipline, my appetite is whetted. Wild horses couldn't keep me from pressing ahead. Instead of the obligation of service to the Lord who bought me, I have the pleasure of a relationship with the Father who chose me. Deep intimacy with my Creator becomes a tangible encounter rather than a distant hope. Best of all—and legalists and systematic theologians may not approve of this—I feel free and have fun right in front of God and everybody. And this, I can finally say, looks a lot like abundant life.

At some point in our relationships with God, we ought to be able to know how he feels without even asking because that's how we feel too.

"EMOTIVATION"

I know Latin is a dead language, but it has been pretty influential from the grave. Quite a few English words are derived from Romance languages—Italian, French, Spanish, Portuguese, and Romanian—which in turn were all derived from the *lingua franca* of the Roman Empire. That means that many words with different meanings that we use in different contexts are, if you take a look at the linguistic family tree, related in the distant past. As it turns out, *emotion* and *motivation* share a common grandparent.

Movare is the Latin word meaning "to move." Its past participle is *motus*, from which we get, via Anglo-French ancestors, the words *motion, motif, momentum, motive,* and *motivate.* A variation on *movare* is *emovare*, which tweaks the meaning a little. It still means "to move," but it's more specific: "to remove or displace." Thanks to the French, the word that comes from *emovare* is *emotion*—something that has the ability to "displace" one feeling or reaction with another, or even to displace us from one place to another. This is why we are able to say, when we've experienced a deep emotion, that we were "moved."

These words are all associated with each other etymologically because the concepts behind them are closely related. We aren't motivated to do something by learning new information. We're motivated by our feelings about the information. When we really want to pursue a certain object or course, we'll persist according to the strength of our desire for it. When we know we *should* do something but don't really have a desire to do it, we may pursue it for a while, but we'll eventually stop. Or we may even train ourselves in a permanent habit, but we'll do it by rote and without enjoyment. In spite of issues of right and wrong or truth and untruth, we will only grow as much as our motivation drives us. And, both linguistically and spiritually, our motivation is inextricably tied to our emotions.

That explains why we fail so often at things we know we should do. If you need an example, think back to your last New Year's resolution. Still at it? I didn't think so. (If you are, it's because you were highly motivated.) This is the reason so many weight-loss plans are purchased and so few people are actually losing weight. Same goes for reading through the Bible in a year, breaking a bad habit like smoking, or going to a gym. Willpower, whether in faith or anything else, is not enough. Having a plan is a start, but the information itself won't get you to your destination any more than a road map will get you to the next town. You have to actually move in the direction the road map shows you. And to do that, you have to want to.

When we stumble, it sounds so much more respectable to say we didn't have the motivation, but that's really just a fancy way of saying we didn't feel like it. Even when you deny yourself and take up your cross, it's because you want to. It may not be pleasurable, but your desire acknowledges that there are greater benefits than immediate gratification. Human beings are wired that way. No matter how emotionless, selfless, altruistic, or objective you try to be, you do what you want to do.

I like to call that "emotivation." (I know it's not a real word, but neither was *movare* at some point in ancient civilization, and judging by its derivatives it seems to have stuck pretty well.) Emotivation isn't really much different than motivation, except that the *e* in front reminds us that motivation is primarily a heart issue. It's that force that connects information and willfulness with our emotional "want" mechanism and allows them to be influenced by it. It comes out as desire—holy desire, we hope—and it can't be satisfied with empty habits and rituals. It pulls us into the things we actually end up doing. If we're following Jesus, we'll do what's true and right because we want to. And if we consistently try to do what's true and right when we don't want to, we'll eventually give it up, get bitter because we can't give it up, or simply have a nervous breakdown. Emotivation, for a Christian, is a Holy Spirit–influenced, emotion-saturated drive to be fulfilled in relationship with God and to live out the gospel. Without it, we can't grow as disciples. And we certainly can't fellowship at a heart-to-heart level with God.

It's important to recognize this dynamic because your heart can go places your mind can't. As Pascal said, the heart has its reasons that reason cannot know. If logic drove the spiritual life, the Bible would have no David volunteering to fight Goliath, no Moses making demands of a hostile Egyptian government, no Ruth lying at the feet of Boaz, no entrance into a Promised Land full of giants, no crumbling walls of Jericho, no prophetic messages or martyrs' deaths, and, worst of all, no Cross and Resurrection. The human mind would not have attempted any of these things on the basis of rational processes. These great faith events happened because people obeyed a God they didn't understand. Why? Because he told them what to do, and they responded because they wanted to. They may not have felt warm and fuzzy about it at the moment—the will and the desire often work together—but they felt something: the gravity of the situation, perhaps, or a passion for the mission. In most cases, they believed it would eventually lead to joy.[9]

That's why reason can never rule the Christian life. None of the above events were *ir*rational, but they were certainly *extra*rational. In God's mind, every one of them made sense. That's because he has all the information and sees the end result. We, however, have finite little brains that could never process all the necessary information without short-circuiting. So, like it or not, God frequently speaks to the heart. When hearts are able to hear the voice of God—fully acknowledging that the voice won't contradict the heart of God as revealed in Scripture, of course—God can do miracles through the people who love him. The human heart can accept things that the human mind will never understand.

PERSPECTIVE MATTERS

Much of your discipleship depends on how you see your emotions. Do you see them as distractions to your relationship with God or helpful aids? Do they obstruct the image of God in you or enhance it? Do they get you off track or alert you of when you need to get back on track? If you are constantly pushing them out of the way and plowing ahead in spite of them, you may be draining yourself of the very fuel you need to draw closer to God. If, in every emotional situation, you ask yourself what your feelings reveal about the God who made you, you may find yourself conformed to the image of Christ faster than you ever thought possible. You may learn to avoid sin because you hate it, not simply because you should. You may realize you love doing God's will because it has captivated your heart, not simply because a Bible verse told you to do something you have no desire to do.[10] You'll end up with a discipleship that integrates all of you into one godly whole.

Let me share an example of how that has worked in my experience. I've found that some books of the Bible are better "absorbed" than deciphered. Leviticus is one of those. For years, reading that book prompted all kinds of questions for me about the relationship of Old Testament law to the Christian life and about the oddity of blood sacrifice actually mattering to a spiritual God. Those are good questions to ask, and I'm glad for the confusion I encountered and wrestled with in Leviticus. But in trying to decipher the letter of the law in that book, I never engaged in the heart of the God behind it.

That changed when I decided to read Leviticus from beginning to end several times. No questions, no notes, no commentaries—just reading. By the third or fourth time through, I noticed that I had begun to feel the weight of human sinfulness and the tragedy of the Fall. Though I still didn't understand the details of sacrifice, the enormity of this solution gave me a sense of awe at the holiness of God and a sense of grief over the holy image we shattered in Eden. As I put myself in the emotional context of the Hebrews in the wilderness, the grace and glory of this covenant began to sink in. My initial attempts to understand the book intellectually interfered with my ability to sense its message. Absorbing the "feel" of Leviticus enhanced my growth dramatically.

As a result of this experience, I'm convinced that when we try to understand the letter of the law and live by it (mind and will), we might fulfill many of the requirements of the law. We won't fulfill all of them, though, and we miss the Spirit behind it. But when we encounter the Spirit, even without understanding, we get not only the Spirit, but also a greater ability to integrate the Word into our lives. The letter (our own mind and will) kills, but the Spirit (the mind, will, and emotions of God) gives life.[11]

Revelation is another part of the Bible that is better absorbed than analyzed. It's a sensory, experiential book that has proven difficult to decipher. That's why we've come up with an abundance of mind-numbing time lines, charts, and end-time predictions that vary not only in minor details but also in major teachings. But try reading

Revelation from beginning to end three or four times in a row, and you'll begin to "absorb" the cosmic epic of God and his fallen creation. You still won't be able to impress people with your knowledge of how and when Jesus is coming back, but you will have tapped into the heart of God in a way that may surprise you. As most people who have been to college can testify, the principle of osmosis never works when placing your head on a chemistry book while you sleep in the library. But when the living Word of God and the living Spirit of God interact with your heart, osmosis is essentially what happens. Instead of truth coming into your head, it begins to flow out of your heart—and you're not quite sure how it got in there.

IT'S AN OPPORTUNITY, NOT A DISTRACTION

In the process of discipleship—following Jesus with an integrated heart, mind, and will—we find ourselves experiencing a wide range of emotions. Before you dismiss them as distractions or try to re-form them into something more "spiritual," try an experiment. Whatever situation may be causing your feelings, see if it parallels a situation God may sometimes experience in his relationship with his people. When you do that, you'll frequently discover a depth to his character that you've never thought of before.

For example, let's say you're Colonel Brandon of *Sense and Sensibility* (see chapter 1), whose heart was ripped open when his true love fell for another guy. You'll need healing for that wound, but before you try to put the hurt out of your mind, meditate on how God felt when his chosen people, the apple of his eye,[12] on whom he had lavished extravagant treasures and promised eternal blessings that no human being has yet experienced, ran off and slept with another idol. And another and another. Again and again.

If you think your jealousy and God's are two completely different emotions, think again. Scripture says otherwise. Its pages are full of adultery metaphors because God inspired those images to describe his heart. As that begins to sink in, you will have bonded deeply with an aspect of God's personality that few people really experience.

If you're a parent, recall the unbridled delight of holding your first child in your arms. There's a reason they call those marvels bundles of joy. You look at that precious being who, at this point, has done absolutely nothing to deserve your love or even respond to it, and all you can feel is overwhelming affection. Hopes and dreams well up within you, and you'd give *anything* to that child—absolutely anything—even if he or she grew up to resent you, ignore you, or betray you. If you've never understood the love and the grace of God, you do now. You've absorbed a theological truth that textbooks cannot teach because your heart has connected with your Father's in a way that identifies with him and draws you closer.

There's no limit to the ways you can do this. Are you in a tedious relationship with a friend or a spouse and praying daily that the relationship changes and grows? Then you have a glimpse of God's patience as he waits for transformation to occur in our lives. Have you grieved over someone who has died without knowing the Lord? Then you've been given a hint of his grief over those who never come into his Kingdom. Have you been given a blessing you never expected? Then, like God, you can rejoice over the generosity of the person responsible for it—and share his joy in arranging it.

This may be a new way of thinking for many of us, but it certainly isn't new to God's people. Isn't this what Paul was doing when he expressed a desire to share in the fellowship of Christ's suffering?[13] I don't think Paul particularly enjoyed suffering, but he was motivated to endure persecution because it was a shared experience with the Savior he had once persecuted. Paul's great desire was to "know Christ." And the means to do that was to subjectively endure what Jesus endured and bond with him over it.

In this way, every emotion we feel, whether positive or negative, becomes an opportunity to connect with God. Those emotional "distractions" we once tried to put behind us because they interfered with our discipleship are actually the common ground between God's heart and ours. At least one aspect of each of our emotional experiences can be tied to a corresponding sentiment in God's dealings with his people. And very frequently, as we look for that parallel, he pulls the veil from our eyes and says something like, "Do you see? This is why sin makes me angry. This is why I'm jealous for your love. This is how much I adore you. This is what heaven's joy is like." And whenever he does that—quite often, if we'll let him—we grow closer to him. Affection between us and our Creator flourishes. We recognize the sympathies he wants to share with us. And our hearts begin to beat with his.

Every emotion we feel, whether positive or negative, becomes an opportunity to connect with God.

the black sheep of the soul

taming the wildlife within

IT WAS THE same at nearly every altar call. Audrey would amble to the front, hankie in hand, and lean on the shoulder of whichever pastor had the duty of greeting her that week. The soundboard technicians would push the volume knobs up a little higher so the musicians could drown out her wails. Members of the congregation would look around nervously to watch the reaction of first-time visitors. *Why can't she control herself?* we collectively but silently lamented. For Audrey, it was the only way she could know that "the Spirit moved her." For the rest of us, it was embarrassing, annoying, and much too frequent—almost as if she couldn't feel that she'd really been to church unless she stained the carpet with a few more tears. Her repentance may have been very genuine, but the regularity of it convinced many people otherwise. Only she and God knew for sure.

Whether we're observing frequent criers like Audrey or the exuberant worshipers common to many of our churches, we feel compelled to form an opinion of them. Our assumption about people wearing their emotions on their sleeves is that they *should* be able to control themselves, and that restraint is an admirable and mature quality that's everyone's general goal. But that's not true, is it? Who said the wild heart needs to be tamed? Who decided that dignity and restraint have anything to do with maturity? Certainly not someone who knew much about worship in the Bible, or who took to heart Jesus' comments about the desirability of becoming like children. Maybe, in God's value system, expressiveness is a sign of maturity. The more undignified someone is, the freer he or she is from the fear of human opinions and the better he or she is able to enjoy God.

I recently saw a church Web site that offered a reasoned approach to faith as an alternative to the overemotional denominations out there. The site cautioned against "too much excess." (Since *excess* already means "too much," I found this to be a creative way to emphasize that we should avoid too much too much.) The implication was that emotional faith isn't really faith at all.

If you ask the average American Christian to name all the qualities of true spirituality he or she can think of, I suspect "real emotion" wouldn't make the list. That's because we think of the über-saints of yore who sat in stark, stone-cold rooms at five thirty in the morning lamenting the fact that they had such little time to pray and whacking themselves with a ruler whenever their thoughts began to wander.

Sure, maybe that's an exaggeration, but we've all got images of what hyperspiritual ideals should look like. By and large, Christians love to have emotions but see them as interferences to growth. The serious disciple must rule them with an iron rod.

This is more than a minor problem. Do you realize what happens when true, God-given feelings are pushed to the background as obstacles to maturity? The opening illustration in chapter 1 from *A River Runs Through It* offers a potent example. Paul, the son with the need to express himself most openly, ends up dead in an alley. He has always been the more recklessly passionate of the two boys. That kind of zest for life can be a powerful force for God's Kingdom when it's welcomed by his people, but usually it isn't. It's significant that Paul is thoroughly bored in church as a boy and usually absent as a man. His heart can't find a way to fit in there. His kind of passion is too volatile and risky for an ordered environment like Reverend Maclean's, so it finds other venues. It seems that Paul's feelings eventually ooze out in some very unsavory places. But they have to ooze out somewhere, and it certainly can't be at church.

That happens a lot. When emotions are marginalized in our faith, they come out somewhere else. Usually that somewhere else is not in the house of the Lord; often it's in lots of bars and lots of beds. It comes out in popular music—you can hear more joy on the radio than you can in a lot of churches—and at sporting events, which, in my experience, aren't very dignified affairs but certainly a lot of fun. And what about a sense of awe, wonder, and mystery? You really don't get that anywhere if you don't get it in God's presence—unless, of course, you

When emotions are marginalized in our faith, they come out somewhere else.

counterfeit God's presence with the idols and occultism that grieve his heart so much.

I have a theory that the church's and society's fear of people getting emotionally out of control has produced a lot of out-of-control people. The art and music that flow out of a person's soul could flow into the presence of God through the community of faith, but the community of faith often clogs up the process. It stops the flow with fine Christian leaders whose hearts aren't connected to God's, so they aren't sensitive to the emotional experience; and it stops the flow by presenting a picture of a God who wouldn't be interested in anyone's feelings anyway. So instead, we have subcultures and drug cultures and pop cultures that are fed by people who just want to spill out their feelings somewhere—anywhere—that helps them feel alive. And a lot of times, their thirst for life drives them to drink something like death—or at least a poor imitation of God's Kingdom.

When those feelings are channeled away from the Kingdom of God and into poor imitations long enough, they become synonymous with the poor imitations. That's why things like dancing, innovative music, drama, and even passionate romance—all very biblical concepts—have, at various times in various cultures, been considered "of the devil." Christians abandoned them for their emotional excesses, so people who were created to dance, experiment with sounds, write or perform dramas, and fall madly in love found ways to do those things outside of Christian fellowship. As a result, many have only known these activities in their secular forms. Dancing and music have become the domain of nightclubs and drug-infested concerts, drama the domain of a sleaze-happy entertainment industry, and romantic passion the domain of an amoral, sex-saturated culture. Now "respectable" society and church leadership have every reason to put a damper on them because they often get people in trouble. "See? We told you so. Feelings lead you astray. Isn't it obvious?" But the result is a false ideal, a hope that one day mature people everywhere will be able to live in harmony without volatile people messing everything up with "too much excess."

BRAVE NEW KINGDOM?

Aldous Huxley believed that humanity's search for utopia, if successful, would ultimately result in the suppression of individuality and emotions. His book *Brave New World* attacked that quest, portraying a stable utopian society as a sterile, empty existence in which people avoid all negative thoughts through programming and recreational drugs, but lose meaningful happiness and fulfillment in the process. This dehumanization is necessary and even desirable in such a society in order to maintain the three highest values, articulated well by the state motto: Community, Identity, Stability.

In spite of the thoroughly humanistic (and anti-Christian) worldview of his book, Huxley was right about the true cost of stability (as human society tends to define stability). A truly stable community (outside of God's Kingdom) requires human beings who function predictably, almost like robots. They can't get too high or too low, they can't act on their emotions without first conforming completely to the principles laid out before them (by which time the emotions are gone anyway), and they can neither prompt nor be affected by change. Individuality—especially the emotional side of individuality—is dangerous.[1]

That's an exaggerated picture that serves a literary purpose in exposing the pitfalls of social manipulation. But in the midst of this futuristic statement on progress and technology, Huxley made a good point about human emotions. Communities, especially large ones, tend to try to govern individuality because, in large part, it's a product of emotions. Our feelings are the most accurate measurement of who we really are. In a society in which stability, peace, and a common purpose are important, emotions tend to get in the way. They can be volatile, which threatens stability; prone to conflict, which threatens peace; and subject to wild tangents, which threatens the mission. They make social groups nervous.

Does any of this sound applicable to the church? It would be grossly inaccurate and unfair to categorize Christian communities as mind-controlling governments, but the dynamic of leaders getting nervous when multitudes get emotional seems very . . . well, familiar. We don't like for the sentimentality of a few to shape the decisions of the whole, for one thing; and nothing makes us want to hammer down our common theology more quickly and emphatically than a highly emotional worship service. Evangelical culture is afraid of its members getting out of control.

The false assumption, of course, is that being "in control" is a viable option. Whose control should Christians, whether corporately or individually, be under? Not the church's control. Anytime historically that the church has exercised tight authority over personalities, the eventual counterreaction has been very messy. (Not to mention that Protestants oppose religious control in principle anyway.) Neither should Christians be under their own individual control. Self-control is a gift of the Spirit, but raw discipline imposed on ourselves is always an empty and desperate battle. No, the only control we want to be under as Christians is Spirit-control, which really isn't control at all. Rather than compulsion, it's the Holy Spirit's influence—his ability to saturate and overwhelm us with his love and his ways—that makes us want to do what we're called to do. So "in control" is an understandable, but false, human value.

"In control" also looks entirely different to the Spirit of God than it does to dignified people. We define self-control as refusing to act on inappropriate desires and always containing emotional extremes. But that's not God's kind of control. Sure, he doesn't want us to act on inappropriate desires—or even have them, for that matter—but his solution isn't to conform us to community standards of personality and behavior. He wants to conform us from within to match *his* character, which includes a full range of emotions. To him, someone can be dancing wildly or weeping profusely and still be "in control."

Most of our heroes of faith wouldn't make it in a brave new world or, to be honest, even in the evangelical community. What would we do with an Isaiah who walks around naked for three years to prove a point?[2] Or an Ezekiel who spends well over a year lying on one side?[3] Or a Hosea who says it's really okay for him to marry a prostitute because God told him to?[4] Or an old man who says God told him to take his only son up on a mountain to sacrifice him?[5] If we had a strong reaction against one of these people who walked incognito into one of our churches and made such claims, we would be opposing the will of God. We would also reveal at least a faint desire for "Community, Identity, Stability." We would expose hints of *Brave New World* within our midst.

God wants to conform us from within to match his character, which includes a full range of emotions.

I'll be perfectly honest. If Abraham and Ezekiel stood next to me at church, I'd look down on them. (That is, of course, unless I actually knew who they were, in which case I'd ask for autographs and throw a couple of "I've always wondered about . . ." questions at them.) I'm really uncomfortable with people who make a scene (Ezekiel) or who make outrageous claims about unrealistic promises (Abraham). Those kinds of people stretch me way out of my comfort zone. And to think: I'm a huge fan of radical faith. But I'm not a fan of *misguided* radical faith, and until I've read about someone's history-changing, supernatural favor in the pages of my Bible, I pretty much assume that's what they've got.

My point is that God frequently provokes in others an emotional response, a strange desire, or an exuberant or gritty faith that rubs us the wrong way. And *that's* the problem with evangelical fear of individuality and emotions. We're called to extremely high standards of holiness, we're on a relentless mission until Jesus returns, and we're designed to live in the unity of the Spirit. Yet the Spirit is radical, unpredictable, and emotional. He doesn't seem to be stacking the deck in our favor when it comes to unity. He always upsets the status quo, which threatens our idea of how holy and united the status quo should be. We don't know how to deal with that.

This is nothing new, of course. All human beings have struggled with the tension between conformity (served best by level-headedness) and individuality (served best by emotional freedom). It has been a constant source of tension in Christian history, but its roots go even farther back than that.

A LONG HISTORY OF CONTEMPT

Zeno of Citium lived three hundred years before Jesus, his life over-lapping with that of Alexander the Great. This Phoenician merchant took an interest in philosophy in his forties, so he left his trade and submitted himself to the teaching of a gruff and grim philosopher who trained him in Cynic thought and an ascetic lifestyle. As his own ideas developed, he began to teach under the covered and columned porticos commonly surrounding Greek marketplaces. Walking up and down these public arcades—called *stoa* in Greek—he taught his pupils that wisdom comes through our ability to control our own emotions and desires. His lectures emphasized *apatheia*—the absence of passion (from which we get the word *apathy*)—and explained how a person can ultimately arrive at tranquility: by indifference to pleasure and pain. Stoic philosophy—named so because of the *stoa* under which Zeno taught—became one of the dominant philosophies of the Greco-Roman world.

Centuries after Zeno, around 4 BC, two very influential men were born. One grew up to embrace Stoic philosophy and popularize it among the masses. Like all good Stoics, he emphasized reason and virtue over emotion. Life, he believed, is essentially a cognitive experience. This philosopher, Seneca, mentored the Roman emperor Nero until he fell out of Nero's favor. He died in AD 65 at his own hand; falsely accused of plotting an assassination, he was ordered to kill himself or be killed. He stoically chose the former, cutting his wrists and bleeding to death.

The other influential man born around 4 BC came to restore the image of God to creation. He died much earlier than Seneca did; also falsely accused, he actually chose to be killed. But before he died his very temporary death, he demonstrated what godliness should look like in human beings. And far from teaching his disciples to deny their emotions and live according to reason and virtue alone, his stated purpose was for them to experience his joy[6] and even to have the full measure of his joy within them.[7] (Let that sink in: the full measure of the joy of an infinite God.) He was known to offer up his prayers with loud crying and tears,[8] but he also endured the Cross for the joy set before him,[9] neither of which would have endeared him to any Stoics. Apparently, the true image of God wasn't worried about embracing emotional extremes.

The Stoics, quite unlike Jesus, are possibly the best-known emotion deniers in the history of Western civilization. Their attempt to divorce the human spirit from emotional extremes has never actually succeeded, and it never will. You can't suppress a God-given nature forever. But it's important to note how influential this philosophy was on early Christianity. It greatly influenced Augustine, who in turn affected Luther and Calvin, who in turn have shaped modern evangelicalism. Seneca, in particular, has been quoted widely throughout Christian history.[10]

Today, a "stoic" is someone who represses feelings and reliably acts according to truth and logic. And while very few Christians would openly describe themselves this way, Stoic thought is awfully similar to the message the church teaches in most of our discipleship instruction: Understanding is important and practical application is essential, but emotions can never be trusted.

Throughout history, ascetics have followed that same principle. From isolated desert fathers who beat their emotions into submission, to late medieval monks who denied every shred of evidence of humanity within them, unemotional discipline has often been considered the essence or the height of Christian spirituality. This hasn't been the case with every ascetic—many medieval mystics were very emotional and had overwhelming ecstatic experiences. But in general, to deny oneself the extremes of life's physical pleasures involves denying the emotions that come with those pleasures, and Christian history is full of examples of disciples who subjected themselves to emotional anesthesia.

The most overt historical attack on emotions came on the heels of the Reformation and the religious and political turmoil it caused. The Age of Reason—or within that age, the Enlightenment— exalted human reason above all other means to knowledge, especially confronting the idea of divine revelation. Religion, after all, had caused a lot of trouble, so it conveniently became a matter of tradition and superstition, not truth. To rational scientific minds, truth could only be determined empirically. If something couldn't be observed in a test tube, literally or figuratively, it couldn't be considered factual. Truth could never be intuitive or subjective. It had to be proven to the five senses by controlled experiments. Truth, in other words, couldn't be felt.

That's an accepted statement in most branches of Christianity today, even though the Bible is comprised almost entirely of the subjective experiences of God's people. The Age of Reason did a powerful number on us. It brought us many valuable benefits, of course— scientific and industrial revolutions; independence movements around the world; liberal democracies in the United States, France, and elsewhere; natural philosophy; and the scientific method, to name a few. But it also falsely posed rationalism against revelation and naturalism against supernaturalism, and it eventually spawned poisons like Darwinism, Freudian psychology, and Marxism. It became the foundation of secular humanism and, not just coincidentally, also trampled on the legitimacy of human emotions.

The result is a society today that often sees spiritual experiences as a superstitious hangover from the medieval era. When you cry in the presence of God, it can be considered overemotional. When you believe God impressed something on your heart, it's delusional at worst, wishful thinking at best, and dangerous all the way around.

When you're at rest in the midst of a crisis, you're in denial. And the number of Christians who approach life this way—rejecting the spiritual validity of emotional experiences—is astounding.

The spiritual backlashes against the Age of Reason have gone in a number of directions: a rise in the popularity of Eastern religions and New Age mysticism; the growth of certain strains of nationalism and fundamentalism, which often react to rationalism by rejecting everything about it; and postmodernism, essentially a philosophical grudge against religious absolutes and cultural conformity. But within the confines of orthodox Christianity, we also see a transition to freer expressions of worship and a desire, especially among younger generations, to impact the culture for Christ. Even there, within the church, there's tension between those steeped in modernism and those open to living out their faith in nontraditional forms. Historical transitions can be messy, even within Christian circles. Actually, *especially* within Christian circles. In matters of faith, tradition easily becomes sacred. When a generation comes along with different emphases—whether in forms like music and worship, or in cultural personality like passionate expression and openness—there's always something of a battle to be fought.

OVERKILL

Why is traditional evangelical Christianity so opposed to emotional experiences? Other than the historical and cultural influences—which are enormous—the immediate cause is a gut reaction to emotional-*ism*. Emotionalism subjugates the mind and the will and becomes the driving authority in a person's life. It *equates* feelings with spiritual experience rather than accepting feelings as a legitimate aspect of spiritual experience. That's an error in the opposite direction of legalism or intellectualism. It's still an imbalance of the spiritual personality. In our efforts to fix that imbalance, we create another one when we relegate emotions to third class.

We're stuck between two alternatives: Let believers experience untameable emotions, or try to anesthetize them so they only have mild ones. Historically, nearly all denominations and leaders—the guardians of the faith who protect the flock— have unwittingly chosen the anesthesia approach. That's not a calculated decision in most cases, just a misguided mind-set. If we assume that emotions are corrupt and misleading, then numbness will always seem safer than excess. You can probably think of quite a few notable exceptions, many of them televised. And among certain ethnic groups, Christian emotionalism is actually quite acceptable, even admirable.

Emotionalism equates feelings with spiritual experience rather than accepting feelings as a legitimate aspect of spiritual experience. It's still an imbalance of the spiritual personality. In our efforts to fix that imbalance, we relegate emotions to third class.

But well-intentioned leaders of most Western evangelical institutions are generally equipped with powerful "sedatives" to help keep their more exuberant sheep well grounded.

Consider, for example, the well-known train illustration with the Word of God being the engine, faith being a boxcar, and feelings being the caboose.[11] The great benefit of that illustration is that it makes new believers aware that though their feelings may change the day after they accept Christ, the fact of God's promise of eternal salvation remains true. It teaches that emotions don't prove whether faith is genuine. That's an important principle, and I certainly don't intend to criticize an evangelism tool that God has used so effectively to bring many into his Kingdom. I'm not by any means arguing that feelings should be the engine of our lives with facts bringing up the rear. But assigning emotions to the unflattering place of a caboose sends a clear message that feelings are the least important aspect of the image of God within us. That's just wrong. The soul is not a hierarchical entity; it's an equal union of different aspects of the divine image.

Nearly every Christian teacher will make a distinction between valid emotions and the excesses of emotionalism. And they're all correct in the sense that someone who bases his or her faith exclusively on emotions is not going to last as a disciple. We've all seen people who commit to Christ on the mountaintops and deny him in the valleys. That kind of believer will be like the seed that falls on shallow soil and withers as soon as the hot sun beats down on it,[12] and the Christian community is right to warn against that danger.

But in our concerns about emotionalism, we throw a very sensitive, tenderhearted baby out with the no-worse-than-average bathwater. Our warnings against emotion-driven faith are always much, much stronger than our warnings against a faith consisting only of ritual disciplines or pure mental assent to the gospel, even though those extremes are equally dangerous. Why are we so selective in our agenda against false faith? Because Stoicism and the Enlightenment, with their treatment of emotions as the black sheep of the soul, have become the lenses through which we view Christian faith and practice. Because the religious tendencies of fallen humanity always drive us toward our own definitions of spirituality. Because divine revelation has been systematized and reinterpreted and objectively defined. Because we can handle theology a lot better than we can handle God. We want him to be predictable.

That's why we try to tame the untameable. Emotions are messy, and we don't like a mess, so we make discipleship a tidy, well-defined package and minimize the role of feelings that aren't tidy or well-defined. In the process, our approach to emotionalism is like spraying the best fruit in the orchard with pesticides strong enough to kill all plant and animal life. Sure, the pests are dead, but so is the fruit. We're left with a field full of deadwood.

Meanwhile, we have millions of unaffected, unconnected Christians attending church out of diligence and duty while finding themselves drawn to emotional fulfillment elsewhere because there's no room at the inn for their feelings. But we don't preach about that very often. Few discipleship resources have sections on meeting emotional needs in Christ or freely expressing feelings in church. None that I know of emphasize the importance of feeling the way God feels. Our teaching continues to aim its heaviest artillery at a peripheral target. And empty Christians everywhere are left to wonder why their faith isn't as fulfilling as it used to be.

SURVIVORS

In spite of the traditional tendency to push emotions into the backseat of our Christian lives, they've played a critical role in the lives of some of our greatest leaders. Take Martin Luther, for example. By his own account, emotions certainly had a part in leading him to faith.

> Though I lived as a monk without reproach, I felt that I was a sinner before God with an extremely disturbed conscience. I could not believe that he was placated by my satisfaction. I did not love, yes, I hated the righteous God who punishes sinners, and secretly, if not blasphemously, certainly murmuring

greatly, I was angry with God, and said, "As if, indeed, it is not enough, that miserable sinners, eternally lost through original sin, are crushed by every kind of calamity by the law of the decalogue, without having God add pain to pain by the gospel and also by the gospel threatening us with his righteousness and wrath!" Thus I raged with a fierce and troubled conscience. . . . At last, by the mercy of God, meditating day and night, I gave heed to the context of the words (Romans 1:17), namely, "In it the righteousness of God is revealed, as it is written, *He who through faith is righteous shall live.*" Here I felt that I was altogether born again and had entered Paradise itself through open gates."[13]

Feelings, it seems, were a critical part of Luther's journey to the kind of faith that changed the course of Christian history.

Jonathan Edwards is perhaps a more surprising example. This Puritan preacher is, in retrospect, considered by modern standards to have been as stern and dignified as any other joyless Puritan, but that's a terribly false perception of who Edwards and the Puritans actually were. Edwards wrote quite a bit about "Christian affections" and played a vital role in the Great Awakening, a powerful revival movement in American history.

Intrigued by his unique combination of scientific rationalism and ecstatic faith, scholars continue to debate whether Edwards should be understood as the last great Puritan or the first American Romantic. . . . Great Awakening preachers were united in their desire to promote what they called a "religion of the heart," through which converts would move beyond mere adherence to moral duties into an ecstatic experience of spiritual grace. Some of Edwards's parishioners were so moved by their conversions that they could not stop themselves from crying out or fainting. Converts at [Gilbert] Tennent's and [George] Whitefield's camp meetings had even more extreme physical reactions, including shouting, shaking, groveling on the ground, and even falling unconscious. Although Edwards worried that the excessive enthusiasm and emotionalism that prevailed at camp meetings could be delusions rather than true conversions, he used some of the itinerant ministers' rhetorical strategies in his own sermons.[14]

This kind of emotional emphasis is very frequently criticized in the present and honored in retrospect. If a Christian leader other than John Wesley said his conversion was validated in part by his heart being "strangely warmed"—that's what Wesley said of his experience on Aldersgate Street as Luther's preface to his commentary on Romans was being read—we would consider that leader's words irrelevant. And it's true that Wesley's heart was warmed because of an objective fact of our justification. But it wasn't warmed *only* by that truth. A spiritual experience was in play, and that experience shaped the course not only of Wesley's life but also of English and American Protestantism. One warmed heart impacted the world.

Luther, Edwards, and Wesley were not the only great Christians of history—or today—to have been powerfully moved by their emotions. Truth and feeling have combined in the lives of many, many people to accomplish the purposes of God. In spite of our cautions, the significance of spiritual feelings is nothing new.

DON'T TRY THIS AT HOME

Let's go back to those articles I mentioned in chapter 2, the ones that are hypercritical of anyone who associates faith and worship with feelings. I read in one of them recently that true worship is based on doctrine—that it's an objective acknowledgment of propositional truth based on a true understanding of God's Word. Seriously.

That sounds very theologically sophisticated, and all who take that advice are sure to develop a better understanding of the God they sing about at church. But the author's implicit definition of "knowing" God is to have theological understanding. It's intellectual. Fact based. Objectively observed and rarely experienced. An approach that's all the rage in an Age of Reason.

I, however, would like to ask that writer if true intimacy in his marriage is based on the legal certificate at the courthouse. Or the photo album from the wedding. Or the ring on his finger. Sure, these things are essential parts of marriage that signify long-term commitment and remind spouses of the vows they made. But husbands and wives don't grow together in intimacy by hanging the marriage certificate on the wall and staring at it together. They don't even grow in intimacy by learning more facts about each other. They connect by sharing emotions.

No one really wants a "doctrinal" marriage, do they? If we took the same arguments we use for non-emotion-based discipleship and worship and applied them to marriage, the divorce rate would rise dramatically. Would you dare state those beliefs to your wife or husband? "Honey, I sure am glad this marriage isn't about feelings. I just want to reassure you that I'm living according to that certificate we signed. I've studied the true meaning of marriage, I understand what it is, and I'm going to act on what I know to be true whether I feel like it or not. Don't worry about a thing." I think not.

Yes, it's true that love is not a feeling, at least not entirely. But if it doesn't involve feelings most of the time, you've got trouble. Love needs to be saturated with an emotional bond that's so intertwined with the rational commitment you made that you can't tell where one begins and the other ends. If it's not, you'll grow old as two separate people enduring vast chasms between you while sleeping in the same household. You won't know how to talk to each other when the kids are grown. You won't hold hands anymore, and you won't cry in each other's arms or laugh at each other's jokes. You'll be living out the commitment of true love without actually having true love.

Yet that's exactly what many teachers advise when it comes to discipleship and worship. "Live your relationship with God according to truth, not feelings. It's great if you have emotions, but they should be the result of your faith. Never focus on them." In marriage counseling, that's what you say when the relationship is critically missing affection. It's remedial, a desperate measure to hold things together until affections heal. At most times in a relationship, it's bad advice.

AN ASSAULT ON THE HEART

I believe emotions have long been under attack by God's enemy because that's how God's people connect with God. Like in a good child-parent relationship, feelings have a bonding effect. It's entirely possible for kids to grow up fully aware of their true position as children in the family, yet never know true intimacy. They can know the family history, attend the family functions, talk about family business, and study all the papers certifying birth. But when emotions are downplayed in a family, connections begin to weaken. When people stop laughing together, playing together, crying together, and celebrating together—sometimes boisterously, and sometimes even excessively—their identity as family members begins to erode.

So it only stands to reason that emotions would suffer evil attacks from the adversary of God—that culture and our own bad experiences with misplaced emotions would conspire to turn us against emotional expression. As often as historical movements have tried to divorce faith from feeling, this must be a major battlefield. The emotional themes so thoroughly embedded in Hebraic and early Christian culture have been sabotaged by an impostor posing as an angel of light. He offers what looks like a more noble wisdom or higher spirituality than we lowly slaves of passion could ever experience. But if we taste of that fruit, we drive a wedge between ourselves and the heart of God.

That's a serious problem for earnest Christians who truly want to know God. The result is that we are more easily drawn toward temptations that make us feel more vibrant and vigorous and enthusiastic about life. If we're discouraged from finding emotional fulfillment and pleasure in the God in whose image we were made, we'll look for that fulfillment and pleasure in lesser relationships, activities, and interests. Then we find ourselves engaged in a battle that pits the mind and the will against the heart, and if we want to be "good" Christians, the heart will have to surrender not to God but to its own internal peers. In other words, we become spiritual split personalities.

In our outward lives, that's a lot tidier. In our soul, it's stressful. Nowhere in Scripture does God seem overly concerned with keeping spirituality conventional and well-contained—consider Jesus' ministry and the Day of Pentecost, for two examples—but he's certainly opposed to its being too stressful. The New Testament makes it clear that Jesus' burden is light[15] and the gospel brings freedom.[16] Wherever the Spirit is, people are allowed to be authentically who they were created to be, emotions and all.

As much as society and the church have historically tried to manage the spiritual individuality of its people, the Holy Spirit keeps pushing us beyond expectations. If the Spirit who dwells within us could be tamed, then we could be too. But we can't. In Christ, the black sheep of the soul is made as white as snow and led out into the open. We were made to feel free—and to freely feel.

CHAPTER 6

avoiding deception and pain
why we don't trust our feelings

SLY, SINISTER, AND so very self-centered, the Vicomte de Valmont plays on the emotions of women with open charm and hidden cruelty. He can manipulate his way into the bedroom with nearly any woman he chooses, and then crush her by moving casually to his next conquest. The only significance of any of his lovers' feelings, in his mind, is in their potential for exploitation. How the women feel in the aftermath is none of his concern.

Valmont's greatest challenge is Madame de Tourvel—a pious and faithful wife who strives to serve God and remain pure. Her reputation for high moral standards intrigues him. If he can break through that wall, it will be the ultimate compliment to his ego. So he maneuvers his way into her life, orchestrates her emotional responses to him, deceives her thoroughly, and violates her virtue. It is the best and worst game he has ever played.

This sinister character in Pierre Choderlos de Laclos's *Dangerous Liaisons* shows how emotions can be manipulated to entice us into evil. Our natural passions can be both ignorant and persuasive, and that's why we don't trust them. Like Valmont, the seductions of our flesh and the enemy of God can orchestrate powerful feelings to deceive us and violate our virtue. Circumstances can swing sentiment in nearly any direction, and sometimes we act on that sentiment.

If you need proof of that, just talk with any advertiser. You've likely seen plenty of commercials that created a mood without disclosing any information about the product. Car commercials aim to make us picture ourselves behind the wheel driving through the beautiful scenery we see on-screen. Cologne and perfume ads try to draw us into a dramatized relationship because they want us to imagine being one of those beautiful people (plus, it's hard to smell the product through the TV). Camera ads focus more on the idealized subjects than on the camera's particular features. That's because the point of most TV spots is to make you feel a certain way, not to inform you.

Though most advertisers employ sentiment to draw our hearts toward a legitimate product, con artists use the same technique to deceive. If a swindler can get the target's sympathies and inspire a vision for the bogus deal, the rest of the scam is relatively easy. That's because emotions are motivating. What seems to point us down the right path can actually lead us willingly, even enthusiastically, into an overwhelming temptation or a subtle trap. A weapon with that kind of force has the potential to destroy us.

FEELING DECEIVED

There are two main reasons we try to avoid emotional extremes, or at least avoid making decisions based on them. One, which we'll look at in more detail later, is avoiding pain. But the first reason that's most obvious to us is that feelings can be so misleading. By contrast, the mind of reason can read God's rulebook, process the information, make logical applications to life, and then dictate to the feelings how the self must act. That process is manageable, observable, and very rational. We don't always live up to our standards that way, but at least we have the guidelines so we'll know when we've violated them. Then we can lecture our emotions into submission and try, try again.

We've already discussed some of the pitfalls of willpower Christianity. It's the way many Christians implement their commitment to Christ, and it's very effective against seducers like Valmont, Satan, and our own deceitful flesh. Step one: Know the truth. Step two: Live the truth. End of story.

Our zeal to guard against deception in the Christian life is valid—critical, in fact. But consider this: When we talk about the unreliability of feelings, what are we saying about our intellect? We're making the implicit statement that our reason *is* reliable. By downplaying emotion, we're elevating the human mind and will as the most stable elements of the soul. If we define "stable" as unchanging, we may be right. But if we define it in terms of reliability, we're fooling ourselves.

The history of Christian thought is a perfect case study. In applying human reason to biblical doctrine, we now have more than 39,000 denominations in the world.[1] Since no two are identical in theology or methodology, only one of them could possibly be perfectly correct, and you and I both know how unlikely that is. That means that at least 38,999 groups of thinkers, all of them approaching the Bible with

By downplaying emotion, we're elevating the human mind and will as the most stable elements of the soul. If we define "stable" as unchanging, we may be right. But if we define it in terms of reliability, we're fooling ourselves.

a generally sincere desire to arrive at truth, have gotten a few things wrong. That's how capable our minds are of objective, reliable reasoning. In other words, they aren't.

If you want a more concrete example about the unreliability of our minds, read several different articles from a variety of media reporting on the same news event. Any contradictions? Any variation in the arrangement of facts from most to least important? Any significant facts included in one that were left out of the other? What you're observing is the varied perceptions that even supposedly objective and professionally trained people can have. Such an exercise is not a great confidence booster for our mental faculties. We all look at things in different ways, even when we're trying to be completely objective. The rational mind is not the authority we wish it to be.

Try an experiment: Remember how many times you have had to admit that you were wrong about something. You were absolutely convinced of something you witnessed, read about, heard, studied, or whatever, only to find out soon after that your perceptions were wrong. I, for example, have been certain that it was going to rain the next day (not a cloud in the sky), that the Atlanta Falcons were going to make the play-offs (they didn't, mainly because they're the Falcons), that I read a particular article in one of our magazines at

Walk Thru the Bible (it never actually appeared in any of our magazines), that a very reliable friend saw two of our acquaintances on a date together (they had never actually met each other), that I had once successfully used cinnamon in a certain soup recipe (I couldn't have, because it tastes nasty now), and that I saw a particular movie with my wife (must have been someone else, she says suspiciously). I have found myself absolutely paranoid in some situations, absolutely oblivious in others, suspicious of people whose words or gestures I later realized I had misinterpreted, and angry at people over an offense that, as it turns out, they never committed. Our minds can play unlimited tricks on us because they are imprecise interpreters of information.

That's why psychology is such a fascinating field of study. Just a quick glance through the *Diagnostic and Statistical Manual of Mental Disorders* published by the American Psychiatric Association reveals more neuroses and psychoses than most of us have ever imagined were possible. Some of them alarmingly describe many of our acquaintances and even ourselves. Almost all of us need some sort of counseling at some point in life because we need help sorting things out. Mental distortions like depression, anxiety, narcissism, paranoia, and delusional thinking are surprisingly common, and they range in degree from mild to severe to extremely pathological.[2] If you've ever studied all the clinically diagnosable types of schizophrenia, personality disorders, and panic disorders, you have to be pretty much convinced that all of God's children have got some kind of issue or another to deal with. My point isn't to make light of mental illnesses and disorders or to determine whether they're chemical or spiritual or some mixture of all sides of our personalities. The point is that our reason is the faculty we most often turn to for an accurate assessment of objective truth. Why? Because emotions are so unreliable. In light of our mental track record, that doesn't seem very rational to me.

Our shaky reasoning doesn't apply only to our own personal perceptions or general systems of thought like theology and philosophy; it also applies to the hard sciences. Consider the well-known words of George Wald, winner of the 1967 Nobel Prize for medicine: "When it comes to the origin of life on this earth, there are only two possibilities: Creation or spontaneous generation. There is no third way. Spontaneous generation was disproved one hundred years ago, but that leads us only to one other conclusion: that of supernatural creation. We cannot accept that on philosophical grounds, therefore *we choose to believe the impossible*: that life arose spontaneously by chance."[3] In other words, we often refuse to believe clear evidence because we have a prior conviction we can't let go of. When reason and will are intertwined, the result is often less than reasonable.

At least once a month, sometimes much more often, I read a news article about a new study that is causing scientists, doctors, and historians to rethink what they once held as absolute truth about a certain issue. That means that at some point in time, they were 100 percent sure about a "proven fact" they were really dead wrong about. There's nothing wrong with incorporating new evidence into your understanding, but our confidence prior to the discovery of new evidence is unwarranted. Environmental scientists, for example, warned us in the 1980s that because of the exploding world population, economic growth would be destroyed by 2000 and we'd experience a global unemployment crisis. In the late 1990s we were warned of an impending disaster known as the millennium bug, Y2K, and the U.S. spent about $225 billion to address it. In the 1920s, scientists predicted another ice age, then warned of serious global warming in the

'30s, then alerted us to the coming "runaway glaciation" in the '70s and warned the government to stockpile food, and now have reached a "consensus" that man-made global warming is a fact, even though more than 10,000 leading scientists disagree with the consensus.[4] Pride leads us to declare an ocean liner "unsinkable" just days before it settles on the bottom of the Atlantic, or to lock up a criminal who was "proven" guilty, only to find out twenty years later that the DNA didn't match. We've seen our false confidence in society's collective intellect shattered again and again with disproved "missing links" and all sorts of prehistoric finds; nutritional benefits (or lack thereof) of foods and additives; psychological patterns and tendencies; historical "facts"; and much, much more. Human reason fails—often.

What's our response when this happens? We certainly don't lament the unreliability of human reason and decide that it should never become the basis for our decisions. Have you ever heard anyone say, "Don't base your life on objective thought; it just isn't reliable"? Me either. We view the multitude of our mental errors as exceptions, and we press ahead in our quest for knowledge.

This is unarguably the right approach to the human mind—to acknowledge its fallibility and continue to develop it as a powerful asset. I'm certainly not trying to diminish its importance. But why isn't that our approach to emotions? When we encounter examples of their unreliability, why do we decide that the flaws outweigh their useful benefits? Why does reason get so much credit, in spite of its repeated shortcomings, and why do emotions get so much flack, in spite of their ability to move us in the right direction? Because the Enlightenment has conditioned us to accept what's observable, to be suspicious of what isn't, to link sentimentality with backwardness, and to elevate rationalism as "progress"—even though it cannot know the things of God.[5]

Yes, feelings are more fleeting than evidence-based information, but they can also alert us to problems that reason would never detect.

The Enlightenment has conditioned us to accept what's observable, to be suspicious of what isn't, to link sentimentality with backwardness, and to elevate rationalism as "progress"—even though it cannot know the things of God.

And yes, they are powerful enough to lead us into disaster, but they are also powerful enough to lead us to amazing victories in against-all-odds battles that reason would have told us not even to attempt. Emotional intuition can prompt someone like Paul to go to Jerusalem against all advice, an irrational but God-ordained act that resulted in his opportunity to go to Rome and declare the gospel before the Empire's leaders. It can provoke a William Wallace to rally a ragtag band of Scots against a vastly stronger English army. It can send a missionary into a hostile tribal culture, warn us of impending danger that no one else sees, and inspire us to worship an invisible God with gusto. Emotional intuition has a noble track record. Our tendency to mistrust it and trust reason instead isn't inspired by God; we get it from a rationalist culture. And I believe that's pretty shaky ground for following Jesus.

Jesus' Take on Reason

So did Jesus, apparently. Every time "reason" is mentioned in the gospels, it's negative. The Pharisees and scribes, for example, missed the Messiah standing in front of them because of their highly trained sense of logic. The most explicit example is when Jesus forgave the sins of a paralytic. "Some of the scribes were sitting there and *reasoning* in their hearts, 'Why does this man speak that way? He is blaspheming; who can forgive sins but God alone?' Immediately Jesus, aware in His spirit that they were *reasoning* that way within themselves, said to them, 'Why are you *reasoning* about these things in your hearts?'" (Mark 2:6-8, NASB, italics added). When they were trying to trip Jesus into contradicting a widely held doctrinal belief, religious authorities were frequently portrayed by the Gospel writers as gathering at a distance to reason, develop arguments, conspire, and force him into a logical conundrum.

The battle between reason and experience recorded in John 9 is almost comical. Jesus gave sight to a blind man, and the entire chapter is devoted to explaining how the Pharisees tried to rationalize the event. They couldn't reconcile the fact that Jesus had broken a well-known Sabbath law yet had the power to heal. A sinner with spiritual power? In another incident, they called that "satanic." In this event, they attacked the man's identity. He must not have really been blind to begin with, they reasoned, and this whole "healing" thing must have been staged.[6] Even the testimony of the man's parents, confirming that their son had been born blind, wasn't enough for them.

Throughout the Gospels, those who approached Jesus mentally and rationally missed him; and those who listened to him at a heart level (like Mary sitting at his feet) or experienced him subjectively (like everyone he healed) received him. A telling example is when two of his disciples who encountered him on the Emmaus road after his resurrection did not recognize him. The Spirit had apparently covered their "eyes." But when Jesus finally revealed himself to their minds—after chiding them for being "foolish . . . and slow *of heart*" (italics added) for not believing—they marveled at how their hearts burned within them as he spoke. It's no coincidence that their intellect was blocked until their affections had testified to his words.[7] The heart can accept facts that reason cannot reconcile to itself.

After this encounter on the Emmaus road, we read that the resurrected Jesus suddenly visits his disciples, who have gathered in a room. They are frightened by his appearance—their troubled hearts have allowed doubts to hinder the faith they want to have[8]—even though some pretty intuitive women have already accepted the fact of his resurrection. As he explains to them how all of Scripture has pointed to his sacrifice, he has to open their minds to understand.[9] Human thought processes can't get a handle on it without supernatural help.

This is the problem with the idea many people have about how God speaks: that "he only speaks to us through the written Word." If that Word is being filtered through a human mind, the potential for bad interpretation is always there. I agree that God won't contradict his written Word, but I'm intelligent enough to realize how unintelligent I am when it comes to applying my intellect to the Bible. I've misinterpreted plenty of passages in the past, even preaching the wrong messages from them. I've known quite a few people who have argued with me about certain points and principles, and sooner or later one of us realizes how completely off base we were in our understanding. Our minds draw all kinds of intellectual fallacies from inspired truth. So if we're listening for God's voice only through our own mental reasoning applied to his Word, we're going to be wrong pretty often.

The only time "reason" is specifically mentioned positively in the Bible is in the well-known invitation of Isaiah 1:18: "Come now, let us reason together." But notice that even in this appeal to be rational, God doesn't want us to do it on our own. This is biblical terminology for "don't try this at home." The prophetic plea is not that God's people be rational, but that they conduct their reasoning *with* him. Our minds must be guided by a spirit of wisdom and revelation that often transcends our own comprehension. We need "the mind of Christ" because, as we've seen, our natural reasoning doesn't understand the things of God.[10] Our brains can't arrive at truth independently of him. Our tendency is to do exactly what Paul warns against: "Professing to be wise, they became fools" (Romans 1:22, NASB). We seriously overestimate the reliability of our own understanding, so we rarely warn people about its dangers.

My purpose is not to fault mental processes. God gave us brains and he expects us to use them. But he doesn't expect them to beat the more intangible, intuitive, and inspired senses into submission.

A WOUNDED FORTRESS

As we've discussed, we tend to zealously guard against the deceptiveness of feelings. But we also employ a much more subtle protection, which can be even more damaging to our hearts. It's that wall we build around ourselves to keep us from ending up disappointed. We quell our emotions because we don't want the devastation of having them remain unfulfilled. It's safer to calm our longings and settle for a sober-minded existence than to ride the waves of desire and end up caught in the undertow. Nobody wants to be crushed, and tempering our feelings is the best way to avoid it.

As I write this, I'm sitting on a plane. The man and woman next to me seem to have struck up a friendship. Both are dog lovers, apparently. The woman remarks that she just doesn't know what she would do if she lost her precious pet. He's been such a wonderful companion. The man responds that he tries not to get too attached to his dogs.

We quell our emotions because we don't want the devastation of having them remain unfulfilled.

It's great having them around, he says, and they serve as good friends, but they come and go too quickly. The more attached you are, the more stress you experience. It's best to like them, not love them, he says.

That philosophy is the complete antithesis of "It's better to have loved and lost than to have never loved at all." I can tell from the rest of the conversation that this gentleman doesn't apply his dog principle to his family members, but many people approach life with that kind of caution. Many hearts have been burned before and are very reluctant and slow to invest their affections.

This reserve taken to extremes is expressed in an old Simon and Garfunkel song. The words come from an isolated soul who has built walls to protect himself. "I have no need of friendship," he sings. Why? "Friendship causes pain." He rationalizes his need to feel insulated, hoping in the lie that he'd be better off without real relationships. "If I never loved, I never would have cried."[11] It's a reaction to a Romeo and Juliet syndrome, where embracing true love results in everyone dying in the end. The implicit admission is that sometimes forbidden love—and all other volatile emotions—are forbidden for a reason. And they are better forbidden at the beginning as a self-imposed prohibition, before the possibility of pain gets too real.

It's interesting that the opposite of indifference—easy, childlike attachment—is associated with immaturity in our culture, while a certain amount of guardedness is identified with emotional maturity. I'm not sure how true that is; it seems to me that if we're to have the faith of a child, as Jesus taught, our culture probably isn't the best authority to define maturity. In the Kingdom of God, maturity is childlike faith with all of its simple beliefs and emotions. It's the ability to be friends with someone after five minutes on the "playground," or to smile at a stranger simply from eye contact. The "I Am a Rock" state of isolation is actually where some people end up, but most of us bounce around somewhere between that and childlike openness. And, according to Scripture, we're to begin and end our lives with the emotional freedom of a child.

If guarding ourselves against pain by holding our emotions in check were a scriptural ideal, we'd never have godly examples like Jeremiah and David. More often than not in the Bible, men and women of God wore their feelings on their sleeves. Did they experience pain? Absolutely—in unison with God. And they also experienced love and joy with him. It isn't possible to have the heads of a coin without the tails, but it's better to have both than to throw the coin away.

The Buddhist Solution

The Stoics and other Greek thinkers tried to throw the coin away. Even longer ago, so did Buddhism. The Buddha was once an Indian prince who had never seen suffering until he ventured off the palace grounds and saw the plight of ordinary people. He left the privileges of royalty to learn about life as it really is, and eventually determined that the source of suffering was the human heart. After all, desire and emotional attachments can't disappoint us if we don't have them to begin with. "If I never loved, I never would have cried" is as good a motto for a Buddhist as it is for a Stoic, an existentialist, or a broken heart. If desire is the source of pain, the best way to avoid pain is not to have desire.

I once lived in a country where Buddhism was the official religion, and one of the highest virtues in that culture was a calm heart that never got too high or too low—or influential enough to affect one's outward disposition. At its heart, Buddhism is a denial of self, and I'm pretty sure it's not the denial of self Jesus talked about when he told his disciples to take up their cross. The Buddhist kind of self-denial ultimately results in a rejection of personhood—complete detachment from any desire or feeling that comes from individuality. In life after life after life, a Buddhist believes he or she can escape the cycle of suffering through greater degrees of detachment. Ultimate detachment is called "enlightenment." (Interesting, isn't it, that the word *enlightenment* is so often associated with the defeat of feelings?) Nirvana, the ultimate "hope" of a Buddhist, is a state of being in which the individual no longer exists because it has been absorbed into the universal whole.[12]

I think that's pretty depressing. In conversations I've had with Buddhists, it boils down to a conviction that life is so incredibly painful that the best option is to completely opt out of it by becoming a nonperson. That may sound outrageous, but if you look at it carefully, you'll notice some similarities with Christian self-denial. Many believers also seek to detach themselves from any hint of their own individuality. It's a "none of me and all of you" theology. The principle is based in Scripture: "New life" is taken to mean our own death on the cross by proxy and our resurrection with the Spirit of Jesus incarnated within us. This desire to be surrendered to God is right and good, but the understanding of what that involves is misguided. God never tells us to have no desires or to be unmoved by our emotions. Even Jesus was swayed by his emotions sometimes, and he certainly had desires, as we'll see more closely in the following chapter. Denying oneself may look different for different people, but it can never mean becoming devoid of all personal preferences in order to be consumed by the Holy Spirit.

That kind of thinking has led to believers classifying every conscious desire or feeling as "self" and rebuking it. I've done that at times in my life, and though it seems like a reasonable approach for getting rid of false and sinful impulses, it's also very effective at quenching the Spirit of God. What if the Spirit gave you your desire to be in sales or to do landscaping or to be an athlete; or to live in San Francisco or Charleston or Des Moines? To deny such desires may seem like the spiritual thing to do at times, but if God wants us to have that "abundant life" Jesus talked about, it only seems sensible that he would work *through* our desires sometimes rather than in contradiction to them. The logical conclusion of the total self-denial approach would be for God to work through us independently of ourselves, without any awareness on our part—because if we're aware of a feeling or impulse, it must be "self." That "jar of clay" Paul talked about would become something of a disconnected robot waiting to be plugged in by its creator. But God has never worked that way with his people. That's not what we were designed for.

Whether our motivation for disconnecting is to make wise, godly decisions or to protect ourselves from pain, it's essentially an attempt to opt out of God's purpose to connect with us as whole individuals. It's an unwitting attempt, to be sure, since no sincere Christian really wants to subvert God's design for his or her life. But God's desire is for us to include the emotions he gives us—the ones that are conformed to his character and ways—into our decision-making, our motivation, and even our obedience. They *can* be an obstacle to wisdom at times, but they're more often an integral part of it.

When we discussed the potential of emotions to deceive, we noted that deception also comes through human reasoning. The same dynamic applies to the potential of emotions to cause us pain. Though feelings do often lead to suffering, there's an assumption behind that principle that suppressing emotions can reduce pain, and that's false. I believe that the constant suppression of the heart by the head is its own kind of pain, a slow, torturous death that hollows out the soul without anesthesia. If detachment worked, fewer existentialists and nihilists would commit suicide. Disillusionment can be excruciating.

Numbness, therefore, is never truly an option for the human soul. Those who have been deadened by their wounds are still conscious of the absence of love and joy, and the consciousness aches. It may not carry the intense pain of heartbreak, but emptiness inflicts just as much torment, if not more. Detachment never accomplishes its purpose.

The constant suppression of the heart by the head is its own kind of pain, a slow, torturous death that hollows out the soul without anesthesia.

THE CULTURE OF THE FUTURE

Most futuristic science fiction includes a representation of some sort of unemotional ideal. Androids make good fighters because they can't feel for themselves. Vulcans make good crewmates because they always depend on logic. Rulers are chosen on the basis of their unswerving allegiance to right and wrong, regardless of human sentiment. War has ceased because societies have advanced beyond the fears and offenses of negative feelings. Scientists have genetically engineered all emotional distractions out of the labor force. In sci-fi's representation of human affections, it's truly a brave new world.

That's one picture of the future, but God's true vision is much different. His ideal is the fulfillment of emotions, not the elimination of them. We see that now, in part, whenever we experience love and joy in raising a child, enjoy a fulfilling marriage, or find satisfaction in bearing fruit for the Kingdom. Ultimately, those emotions won't come mixed with any of the unpleasant ones. There will be no weeping in heaven, but there will be joy and celebration. No one will need to counsel broken hearts in the Kingdom because love there will never die. War will be over, and the comfort of peace and security will reign. No one will be deceived by emotions—not because emotions are quelled, but because all emotions will be true. Kingdom culture will be as festive as a wedding banquet.

The Bible's response to emotional detachment should be self-evident: "Those who sow in tears shall reap with shouts of joy" (Psalm 126:5). Both extremes are covered in one sentence, and they're connected to each other. You want joy? Be willing to sow tears. You want to avoid tears? You'll also forfeit joy.

Though Jesus told us to deny ourselves, he never instructed us to deconstruct the personalities he gave us. He wants us to be made in his likeness, which, as we will see in the next chapter, is a very emotional likeness. We need to guard against deception without eliminating the power and purpose of emotions in our lives. We shouldn't go out of our way to seek pain, but we must realize that we, just like God, will feel it. If we, like Paul, want to share in the resurrection of Jesus, we will also need to fellowship in Jesus' sufferings.[13] That means we'll actually need to experience some of them. The highs and lows of human experience are found in the gospel, and they can't be avoided without rejecting the fullness of the gospel itself.

CHAPTER 7

for the joy set before him

the emotions of Jesus and his people

IN MANY WAYS, it's a great picture of the gospel. Princess Aurora lies perpetually sleeping in the castle, the victim of an evil curse. Her only hope is for true love's kiss to wake her, but her true love, Prince Phillip, is in chains in the dungeon of the wicked queen Maleficent, who will do anything she can to keep him away from Aurora's lips. The only way he'll be able to find her is to fight an epic battle against the epitome of evil—and win.

You probably know the story, even if you've never seen *Sleeping Beauty*, Disney's adaptation of the Grimm fairy tale. You know the ending because, in fairy tales, princes don't remain in the dungeon and lament the unlikelihood of finding their true loves, princesses don't remain asleep forever, and curses don't succeed, even when it takes an epic battle to break them.

With a little help, Phillip manages to escape. He uses a magic sword and shield in hand-to-hand combat against the sorceress, who has turned herself into a massive (and very ugly) fire-breathing dragon. Over rough terrain, through thorns, and at one point leaning backward over an enormous chasm, Phillip fights valiantly. Desperation leads to such extremes. This battle simply *must* be won. His true love must be awakened.

Finally, Phillip's sword pierces the dragon's heart and she suffers an earthshaking death. Phillip runs to Aurora's bedchamber, kisses her on the lips, and the couple dances their way to "happily ever after."

Prince Phillip is, in the world of fiction, the anti-Spock. Rationalists don't appear in epic romances unless they're portrayed as villains. That's because everyone is pulling for hearts to be fulfilled, and that can't happen if logic rules the day. Great victories require great sacrifices, which in turn require great emotional investments. That's how the world was designed.

That's also how God redeemed us. Jesus made a great sacrifice of epic proportions to defeat the wicked dragon who had put us under a curse. Many people miss the romance of redemption and use the Cross as an example of doing what's right in spite of our feelings. Like Jesus, who sweated drops of blood the night before the crucifixion because he really didn't want to go through with it, we are to say, "Not my will but yours," and obey anyway. But that's not the whole story of the Cross.

That partial picture looks a lot like Vulcan Christianity. The greatest example of Mr. Spock's approach to life came in one of the original Star Trek movies—*The Wrath of Khan*. In the climactic scene, the starship Enterprise is a sitting duck, completely vulnerable to an impending explosion. Its disabled engine needs a quick repair to regain warp power and speed away, and all that's needed is a crew member to enter the reactor room. The only problem is that anyone who volunteers for the job will be exposed to lethal amounts of radiation. He'll die within minutes.

That's a hard choice for a human to make, but not for a Vulcan. Against the protests of Doctor McCoy, Spock locks himself in the reactor room and restores the power. Dying of radiation, he looks through the window and tells his old friend Captain Kirk not to mourn. "The needs of the many outweigh the needs of the few, or the one," he says. This sacrifice, though painful, was only logical.[1]

This is how many people perceive the Cross of Christ: Jesus wrestled with his emotions in the garden of Gethsemane, but the will of God won. But that's not how the writer of Hebrews saw it. Though Jesus offered up his prayers "with loud crying and tears" (5:7), he ultimately endured the Cross "for the joy set before him" (12:2, NIV). It may have made logical sense to go to the Cross, but that wasn't Jesus' motivation. He went for the joy it would ultimately result in.

Don't miss the significance of that. It may come across simply as a passing observation near the end of Hebrews, but there's a powerful principle behind it. Jesus denied immediate emotions of grief and suffered the cross for another emotion—one that would deeply satisfy and last forever. His sacrifice was neither a Vulcan decision of logic nor a sterile decision of willpower, though both could certainly have applied. The real factor, the deciding motivation, was joy. You can endure a lot when you know the celebration will be worth it.[2]

Jesus passed his emotional priorities down to his disciples too:

- "These things I have spoken to you so that My joy may be in you, and that your joy may be made full" (John 15:11, NASB).

- "Until now you have asked for nothing in My name; ask and you will receive, so that your joy may be made full" (John 16:24, NASB).

- "These things I speak in the world so that they may have My joy made full in themselves" (John 17:13, NASB).

- "Truly, truly, I say to you, that you will weep and lament, but the world will rejoice; you will grieve, but your grief will be turned into joy" (John 16:20, NASB).

The list could go on, but Jesus' emphasis is clear. He could have said, "Ask and you will receive, so that God may accomplish his purposes in you," but he didn't. He could have taught, "I have given you these instructions so you'll know the right things to do," but he didn't. The salvation and discipleship he preached were not simply for the sake of getting saved and being disciples. Our redemption isn't primarily a "do things right" issue; it's a "have my joy" issue. The wedding of the Bridegroom and bride isn't for the sake of the ceremony; it's for the joyful communion that results from it. From beginning to end, the gospel points to an eternal dance à la Prince Phillip and Princess Aurora.

Jesus denied immediate emotions of grief and suffered the cross for another emotion—one that would deeply satisfy and last forever.

What does it mean to have joy? It means living with a sense of fulfillment, abundance, satisfaction, and—dare I say it?—even pleasure.

Pleasure is almost a dirty word in some Christian circles, frequently coupled with other words that increase our contempt for it—"passing pleasure" or "guilty pleasure" or "wanton pleasure." But pleasure is a thoroughly biblical aspect of God's Kingdom,[3] and he wants us to experience it. Godly pleasure is applied to the right things in the right way at the right times. Joy celebrates pleasure. In fact, joy celebrates everything good. It's the climate of the Kingdom.

FEELING HEROIC

How many heroes, whether in fiction or real life, do you know who were unmoved by emotion? Probably not many. In fact, many reluctant heroes don't get involved until someone ticks them off or a true love is in need. The logical necessity of their intervention is not enough to move them; rather, they are thrust into action when their feelings are provoked.

Han Solo is a reluctant hero. He has never been more than a mercenary—interested only in his own profit—until the end of the first Star Wars movie, when he has a change of heart and joins the rebel alliance. In the beginning scenes of *The Empire Strikes Back*, the second movie in the series, Han has plans to leave the alliance. But three things happen to convince him otherwise: Princess Leia, whom he loves, disapproves; his good friend Luke is missing; and the evil Empire attacks. None of these three conditions alone is enough to change his mind, but the combination is irresistible. A romantic relationship, a friendship, and the nerve of an evil empire assault Han's emotions from three different angles, and he is stirred to action. The hero isn't swayed by sensibility; he is swayed by his heart.[4]

That's why most Hollywood depictions of Jesus are so ridiculously false. In most Jesus movies, he walks around like a zombie and speaks in monotone. His eyes are always looking away into the distance—misty, serious, and sad. This, apparently, is the height of spirituality according to our cultural perceptions. He's as austere as a monk, only more so. He's as calm as a Zen Buddhist, only more so. He's as serious as a doctor diagnosing cancer, only more so. And he's very inexpressive.

I know several people who were pleasantly shocked when the adult Jesus in Mel Gibson's *The Passion of the Christ* laughed playfully with his mother. That's not what we're used to seeing in our mind's eye. Jesus was surely much more religious than that, we think—as though the God who long ago created humanity's sense of humor accidentally incarnated himself without one. After all, if you're dealing with a suffering world and eternal issues, you pretty much have to do it with a straight face, right?

By this point, we should all be aware of how unreliable our religious instincts are. Our definitions of piety are often far from God's. As C. S. Lewis said, "Joy is the serious business of heaven." That's where true laughter comes from. So it only makes sense that Jesus might have surprised his mom with a friendly splash of water and laughed about it, or that he told a few jokes when he and the disciples were resting from a busy day of ministry. All work and no play not only makes Jesus a dull Savior, it also turns him into something less than human—which sort of misses the whole point of the incarnation. A God who rejoices in heaven wouldn't send his likeness into the world without the ability to smile.

THE *EXACT* IMPRINT

The writer of Hebrews says that Jesus is "the radiance of the glory of God and the exact imprint of his nature" (1:3). By implication, that means we can learn a lot about God's emotions by looking at Jesus.

So how did Jesus feel? At times he was moved with compassion and overwhelmed with grief. Matthew and Mark describe his travels from town to town healing the sick. "When he saw the crowds, *he had compassion* for them, because they were harassed and helpless, like sheep without a shepherd" (Matthew 9:36). The feeding of the four thousand wasn't just for the purpose of astounding people with a miracle. It met a need. Jesus called his disciples to him and said: "*I have compassion* on the crowd, because they have been with me now three days and have nothing to eat" (Mark 8:2). A leper came "imploring him," believing that Jesus could cleanse him if only he was willing. Was he? "*Moved with pity*, he stretched out his hand and touched him" (Mark 1:41). Two blind men stood by the side of the road and cried out loudly enough to annoy the crowd. Jesus' response? "Jesus *in pity* touched their eyes, and immediately they recovered their sight and followed him" (Matthew 20:34). When Jesus saw a widow at the funeral of her only son—the last relative who could take care of her—"*he had compassion* on her and said to her, 'Do not weep'" (Luke 7:13). Luke paints an emotional picture of Jesus' final approach to Jerusalem: "When he drew near and saw the city, *he wept over it*" (Luke 19:41). The God figure in his parables—a merciful lender and the prodigal son's father—was portrayed as compassionate even when insulted by grievous offenses. And in one of the most descriptive passages about Jesus' emotions, he was profoundly emotional at the gravesite of Lazarus. "When Jesus saw [Mary] weeping, and the Jews who had come with her also weeping,

All work and no play not only makes Jesus a dull Savior, it also turns him into something less than human—which sort of misses the whole point of the incarnation.

he was deeply moved in his spirit and greatly troubled" (John 11:33). The exact imprint of God wept, not because he was at a loss for what to do, but because his feelings lined up with the feelings of his people. And as he came to the burial cave itself, he was *"deeply moved again"* (John 11:38). The deep pathos of God incarnate bleeds from the pages of the gospels.[5]

Compassion may not be an unfamiliar emotion from Jesus—even Hollywood has attempted to capture that one, though they haven't balanced it with his other displays of emotion. Regardless, there's a full, unembellished expression of both sympathy and empathy in the biblical Jesus. It's as though the feelings of an infinite God are flowing through a finite body because the body can't contain them. Jesus is anything but detached.

That's also clear in his anger. A few verses after he wept over Jerusalem, Jesus drove the money changers out of the temple with a violent display of outrage. If someone came into one of our churches and started turning tables over and shouting about how hypocritical we can be, we'd consider that person very unstable, not at all spiritually mature, and probably worthy of jail time. Yet this is an accurate emotion and a well-founded reaction of the imprint of God.

It isn't the only example of Jesus' anger. When he healed a man with a withered hand on the Sabbath, he drew the ire of the synagogue leaders. The wording of the passage helps us picture a pregnant pause. Knowing the leaders' intent to accuse him of wrongdoing, Jesus asked them if it was lawful on the Sabbath to do good or to do harm. But the leaders were "silent." And in their suspenseful silence, in this moment of decision in which righteousness is pitted against self-righteousness, Jesus "looked around at them *with anger, grieved at their hardness of heart"* (Mark 3:5, italics added).

That attitude continues throughout his ministry. You don't call a group of authorities "a brood of vipers" in a spirit of gentleness and compassion.[6] Neither do you pronounce a multitude of woes on them—"hypocrites," "blind guides," and "whitewashed tombs," to name a few of his choicest epithets—in an effort to arrive at a peaceful compromise.[7] The recipients of Jesus' angry declarations considered him insulting and rude.[8] And this, says the Bible, is the exact representation of God.

We generally think of these emotionally volatile attitudes as ungodly. After all, the rest of the New Testament frequently talks about the characteristics of sin: "Let all bitterness and wrath and anger and clamor and slander be put away from you, along with all malice," Paul writes in one exhortation among many that draws a distinction between unredeemed attitudes and our new life in Christ (Ephesians 4:31). He even includes "fits of anger" as something that would disqualify us from an inheritance in the Kingdom of God (Galatians 5:20-21). But Paul also writes pointedly of the wrath of God and by no means considers appropriate anger itself a sin.[9] The issue is not whether we have negative emotions, but whether our negative emotions are right and consistent with God's character. And in Jesus' case, they obviously are.

The issue is not whether we have negative emotions, but whether our negative emotions are right and consistent with God's character.

This harsh picture of the Son of God needs to be balanced with his usually calm and joyful demeanor. Immediately after another pronouncement of woe against two unrepentant cities, he went on to declare to a crowd that he was "gentle and lowly in heart"

(Matthew 11:29). Every one of his beatitudes begins with "blessed are. . .",[10] and the sense of this blessed proclamation is arguably best translated as "how *happy* are the . . ." These blessings are not some intangible spiritual benefit that *may* only be revealed in the heavenly Kingdom but genuine happiness and joy—even an air of celebration—that come from righteous attitudes. The beatitudes are counterintuitive—no one really expects the poor in spirit, the meek, the persecuted, and so forth to be happy—but they aren't hyperspiritual mysteries. Those who live them actually experience pleasure from them.

I've often heard people say that God's goal isn't to make us happy. That statement is directed at people who act as if whatever makes them feel good at the moment must be God's will, and in that sense, it's a great observation. But scripturally, we can say with confidence that God's ultimate goal for us *is* to make us happy. He wants us to experience the blessedness and joy of his Kingdom. He created us to share his wealth of satisfaction, and he offers us "pleasures forevermore" (Psalm 16:11). It may not always be an immediate pleasure, and it may not come by the same means we expect it to, but that's where he's bringing us. It's all about the joy in the end. "Happy" is very high on his list of priorities.

You'll notice that though many of Jesus' parables end with weeping and gnashing of teeth, others end with joyous celebration. This sounds suspiciously like an emotional gospel, with truth and feelings all wrapped up together. God's ultimate goal in this gospel is the kind of festive attitude present at a wedding banquet or a party in honor of a prodigal who returns. There is *much* joy in heaven over one sinner who repents, and that joy surely spills over into the hearts of those on earth who are able to whoop it up—in an appropriate Christian spirit of whooping it up, of course.

As we have seen, Jesus promises quite a bit of joy to his disciples. It would be negligent not to take him up on it.

Don't Act on Your Feelings?

The biblical portrayal of Jesus undermines our never-act-on-your-feelings philosophy of discipleship. Jesus clearly acted on his feelings. He was moved with compassion, he turned tables over in anger, he pronounced woes and blessings in something other than a monotone voice and with other than a straight face, and he treated his followers with great affection, inviting them into his joy. And, don't forget, he made the ultimate sacrifice—in spite of loud crying and tears and the deep distress of Gethsemane—because of the joy set before him. He was both purpose-driven *and* passion-driven, and he never told anyone to separate the two. His life ought to settle the question once and for all whether it's okay to act on feelings. *Okay* to act on feelings? It's imperative! Jesus did.

If we're being transformed into the likeness of Christ, we'll act on our emotions too. We'll want to make sure that our feelings line up with God's; that's part of asking him to continually fill us with his Spirit. But when our emotions do fit the character of our Father and ebb and flow with the breath of his Spirit—we'll discuss the discernment necessary for that later—we can feel free to be motivated by them and even to base our behavior on them. In that light, acting on our feelings is a godly thing to do.

THE PHILIPPIAN SPIRIT

There are plenty of scriptural examples of emotion-infused ministry in the Bible, but the book of Philippians may distinguish itself as Scripture's epicenter of joy. In that short letter, the words *joy* and *rejoice* are specifically mentioned seventeen times, and the general attitude is even more pervasive. As far as I know, Philippians is one of the most emotional letters in antiquity. "It is right for me to *feel* this way about you all," Paul writes, "because I hold you *in my heart.* . . . How I *yearn* for you all *with the affection of Christ Jesus.* And it is my prayer that *your love* may abound more and more" (1:7-9, italics added). Immediately after this comes a prayer for the Philippians' understanding, but note how much emotion-oriented material precedes that. Paul never gives the impression that emotion is based on their understanding, but that the two are intricately connected. The affection and love must abound together "with knowledge and all discernment" (1:9), and if word order is any indication, the affection and love are primary. Paul goes on to write about his choice to rejoice, his eager expectation and hope that he will be unashamed and courageous, and his confidence that the church will progress in joy.[11]

If Paul were preaching in a pulpit today, that kind of talk might be considered an emotional appeal, which would probably get him on TV but cost him a lot of respect. But the apostle doesn't shrink back from it. His emotional intro sets up his main purpose for writing, which apparently was to settle a spirit of contentiousness rising up among the Philippian believers: "If there is any *encouragement* in Christ, any *comfort* from *love*, any participation in the Spirit, any *affection* and *sympathy*, complete my *joy* by being of the same mind, having the same *love*, being in full accord and of one mind" (2:1-2, italics added). If you didn't notice how unusual that thought progression is, let me make it clear: Paul is actually appealing to emotions—encouragement, comfort, love, affection, and sympathy (with the Holy Spirit firmly and suggestively planted right in the midst of that list)—*as a basis for becoming like-minded.* Paul insists that the mind conform to the emotions.

Current evangelical thought does exactly the opposite: We insist that emotions conform to the mind. Not only do we reverse Paul's argument, we even criticize it harshly when we see it in anyone not named Paul. But Paul was not reluctant to set emotions as a foundation and then appeal to them as a basis for understanding.

There's much more to Philippians than this, as most people who have memorized a few verses of the Bible can attest. One of the best known passages about anxiety is found in this letter, and it's filled with the vocabulary of feelings: "*Rejoice* in the Lord always; again I will say, *Rejoice.* Let your reasonableness be known to everyone. [As in the Philippians 2 passage, reason rests on an emotional foundation.] The Lord is at hand; *do not be anxious* about anything, but in everything by prayer and supplication *with thanksgiving* let your requests be made known to God. And the *peace* of God, *which surpasses all understanding*, will guard your *hearts* and your *minds* in Christ Jesus" (4:4-7, italics added).

That's pretty clear. Anxiety is to be conformed to the peace of God. That peace happens to trump understanding because understanding won't connect us to the Spirit. And this peace that the Spirit gives will guard both our hearts *and* our minds in Christ.

Anxiety, distress, peace, joy, eagerness, confidence, courage, comfort, affection, sympathy, love, concern, and kindness—all are specifically mentioned in a letter to the church that Paul seemed to consider more mature than all the others he corresponded with. And the mind? It (including the words that hint at it) is applied to the Philippians in only nine verses—and then only in equal (or subordinate) partnership with matters of the heart[12] or as an instruction for those who may not be thinking correctly.[13] Emotional words vastly outweigh cognitive words in the letter. This, according to Paul, is how the Spirit of Jesus affects a church.

Philippians isn't the only passage in Paul's letters in which emotions figure so prominently. Try reading 2 Corinthians sometime for a remarkable interplay between emotions and understanding. In chapter 7 alone, there's specific mention of joy, grief, sorrow, fear, regret, pride, boldness, zeal, and comfort. "You are in our hearts," Paul tells his readers, "to die together and to live together" (7:3). In other parts of that emotional letter, Paul explains the comfort of God, with which we comfort one another in our sufferings;[14] the fact that God isn't really interested so much in giving for the sake of giving, but that he loves a *cheerful* giver because giving is about the motive rather than the understanding and the action;[15] that Paul feels "a divine jealousy" on behalf of God for his Corinthian bride;[16] and that his revelations and visions of truth came wrapped in a package of ecstasy and elation.[17] Truth is integral to every one of his points, but truth never pushes feelings into the backseat. If anything, these Spirit-inspired feelings are the basis of Paul's appeal to conform to truth.

THE SPIRIT OF JESUS

It's clear from the New Testament and Scripture as a whole that the Holy Spirit inspires feelings, and that sometimes he inspires those feelings before he provides understanding.[18] In many places, Christians are urged to increase in understanding, so it's clear that the mind is critically important. But the early church was profoundly filled with awe, zeal, hope, joy, peace, gratitude, love, and all kinds of emotion-saturated attitudes simply by accepting the Spirit of Jesus, whether or not they understood what was happening. And more often than not, they had to choose to accept or reject their emotional experiences before they figured them out theologically. Those who *did* suspend belief until they figured out the theology of it all—the priests, Sadducees, and court of law in Acts 4–6, for example, as well as the Christian Pharisees of Acts 15—usually missed the Spirit altogether.

What does that mean for us today? It means that sometimes we will have to accept a move of the Spirit before we understand it. We will have to trust the Spirit to guide us not only through our understanding of the Word, but also through the gut-level impulses that are spiritually appraised. It means that we can't have the peace that passes understanding if we insist on understanding; and that the life of discipleship is built around love, joy, peace, patience, and a host of other emotive qualities that can function quite well without the mind's approval. Most of all, it means that if we want to be conformed to the image of Christ, we will have to act on feelings like compassion and anger when they line up with God's heart. And when we take up our cross and die daily, it's okay—even imperative—to do it for the joy set before us.

Truth is integral to Paul's epistles, but truth never pushes feelings into the backseat. If anything, Spirit-inspired feelings are the basis of Paul's appeal to conform to truth.

synchronizing

feeling the divine pulse

I SAW IT WITH my own eyes. The lady in the seat next to me had a gap where a tooth had once been. We were led in a congregation-wide prayer for healing, and when she smiled afterward, the gap was gone. A perfectly formed tooth filled the space. She let another woman try to wiggle it with her finger, and it didn't budge. She had tears in her eyes. It was real—no doubt about it.

I told a friend about it later. "I don't see how that would glorify God," he said. After all, it was purely cosmetic. Too trivial for God. She must have slipped a fake in when I wasn't looking. Couldn't have been a miracle, he said. I even told my dentist about it the next time

I was in the office. "Oh, really," he said. "That's interesting." Same response he'd have given if I'd been on the gas.

It's interesting to observe the various reactions Christians display when they hear a report of a miracle. Some people accept the report as true and immediately rejoice. Most, however, first question the source or try to think of a naturalistic explanation, even when they long for a supernatural experience.

For most of my life, I've fallen into the latter camp. Having witnessed miracles and been exposed to many other reports of them lately, however, I'm having to retrain my mind. It has occurred to me, especially in scouring the Bible for the scriptural basis of this book, that those who eye miracles with suspicion are never spoken of favorably by inspired writers.[1] That's a little disconcerting, considering the skepticism with which we approach the world today.

But skepticism has always been the order of the day, hasn't it? It isn't an Age of Reason phenomenon. The women who went to Jesus' tomb were too shocked to believe at first, but it didn't take them long to embrace the Resurrection. The disciples, on the other hand, seemed to take some persuading. And when Jesus came to them, he rebuked them for not believing the women's testimony.[2] Their report of a miracle—even one explicitly prophesied on multiple occasions by the Son of God himself—was greeted with skepticism.

That has been true throughout Christian history, even from the earliest days. The apostles encountered many rejections for their claim that a man was raised from death.[3] Paul at one point declared that he was on trial for the resurrection of the dead.[4] The Pharisees did a lot of fact-checking to disprove some of Jesus' miracles (in particular, the healing of the blind man as recorded in John 9), but they could never do so. In each case, suspicion was considered wise by human standards—"discerning," we like to call it to sound scriptural and spiritual—but disobedient by God's standards.

As alarming as that is to most of us discerning Christians, let's consider why God might view our suspicion with the disfavor he does. When God does a supernatural work, what's the attitude in heaven? Joy. When we withhold our joy until our minds are satisfied, we're actually choosing not to adopt the attitude of heaven. The angels are throwing a party over God's generosity, and we're not joining in. Why? Because we don't want anyone making a fool of us.

Those who eye miracles with suspicion are never spoken of favorably by inspired writers. That's a little disconcerting, considering the skepticism with which we approach the world today.

Nowhere in the Bible are we cautioned not to let people make a fool of us. Plenty of proverbs tell us not to *be* fools, but they use God's definition of foolishness, not man's. The world will always consider faith somewhat naive. In fact, if people don't consider us fools from time to time, we're not really living according to the gospel. That's why Jesus was so careful to tell his disciples to rejoice in the face of insults;[5] he knew insults would come. And that's why Paul was led to say that all who desire to live a godly life in Christ will be persecuted;[6] he knew the world's contempt for the ways of Jesus. But he also believed that even the foolishness of God is wiser than the wisdom of men.[7] And Jesus made clear that those zealous for their own reputation would not be fit for the kingdom.[8]

So we really have no excuse for rejecting the celebration in heaven because our minds just aren't sure God would intervene supernaturally in the affairs of human beings. That's one example of not conforming emotionally to God because the mind gets in the way, and there are many others. We're so busy exalting the virtues of discernment that we miss the simplicity of faith, along with all the peace and joy that comes with it. We can talk ourselves out of believing just about anything God does. While we're waiting for the airtight proof of his Spirit's obvious work, he's allowing plenty of room for our skepticism so we'll have to make a spiritual choice. Believe the Spirit's power—or find a natural explanation for it? Trust what the heart already knows—or subdue the heart in favor of the mind's suspicions? Pursue our own dignity—or join in what might be God's celebration of a miracle? It's almost a daily choice for every believer, and we've been conditioned by society and our own teaching to rely on explanations. That puts us squarely in the camp of the Pharisees, who refused to rejoice over what they saw with their own eyes.

In every area, not just joy, God means for us to share his emotions. He designed us for relationship, and relationships consist of emotional bonds.

BUBBA-GUMP THEOLOGY

"My given name is Benjamin Buford Blue, but people call me Bubba." That is Forrest Gump's introduction to his best friend in the army. From the rigors of boot camp to the horrors of Vietnam, Forrest and Bubba grow close enough to know quite a few details of each other's lives. Bubba's past experiences seem to be rather one-dimensional. His family's business is shrimp, and he can seemingly talk forever about the multiple ways to serve it up. "You can barbecue it, boil it, broil it, bake it, sauté it. . . . There's shrimp kabobs, shrimp creole, shrimp gumbo, pan-fried, deep-fried, stir-fried, pineapple shrimp, lemon shrimp, coconut shrimp, pepper shrimp, shrimp soup, shrimp stew, shrimp salad, shrimp and potatoes, shrimp burger, shrimp sandwich . . ." and on and on and on.

For his part, Forrest is genuinely interested in hearing all about shrimp. The bond that develops between the two friends grows deeper and deeper, not just over shrimp, but over the trials and tribulations of menial service and violent fighting. When both of them are injured, Forrest feels attached enough to Bubba to run into a blazing jungle to carry his friend out, even against direct orders. Like a Savior bent on healing on the Sabbath, he risks his own life and the ire of a lieutenant to save a friend.

In his dying breaths, Bubba laments the unfulfilled vision of owning his own shrimp company. Later in the movie, after Forrest is released from the army, he decides to go to Bubba's home in Bayou la Batre, Alabama, buy a shrimp boat, and live out his best friend's dream through the Bubba-Gump Shrimp Company. He knew nothing about the shrimp business before he met Bubba, and he knows very little about it years later. But his passion for his friend overrides all inexperience, costs, and logistical difficulties. He can't let Bubba's dream die because their hearts are forever connected.[9]

That's how relationships work. Shared experiences create bonds, and bonds deepen over time. The closer two people grow, the more they share each other's feelings and dreams. When one suffers, the other suffers, and when one rejoices, the other does too. And if their hearts were placed next to each other, they would begin to beat in the same rhythm.

The application for our relationship with God should be obvious. If we spend a lot of time with him, enjoy his company, listen to his stories, share life experiences, and tell him about all of our problems and passions, we'll notice the rhythmic pulse of friendship getting stronger. His plans will become our plans, his heart will affect ours, his purposes will transform us, his thoughts will seem more natural to us, and our bond will grow deeper.

Amazingly, however, that's not all there is to it. This isn't a one-sided transformation. No, I'm not suggesting that God changes, especially not in his essence. He is the unchanging God from age to age. But for some reason, he has made himself vulnerable to the feelings and desires of his people, and the more our hearts begin to beat in sync with his, the more sympathetic he becomes to our passions. His dreams affect us, and our dreams affect him. The relationship is mutually moving.

God's dreams affect us, and our dreams affect him. The relationship is mutually moving.

That's essentially what Psalm 37:4 is getting at: "Delight yourself in the LORD, and he will give you the desires of your heart." It's also the promise of Jesus: "If you abide in me, and my words abide in you, ask whatever you wish, and it will be done for you" (John 15:7). Where a heart connection flourishes in a relationship, the understanding and the actions will follow.[10] God reveals to us a divine secret: His will is drawn like a magnet to a heart that beats with his.

With that in mind, ask yourself some penetrating questions. Are you angry at the same things God gets angry about? Are you jealous for his bride and zealous for his Kingdom? Do you rejoice when he rejoices? Do you weep over Jerusalem and every other city that has rejected his truth? Are you at peace when he gives you rest? Are you as content with his mission as he is? In other words, to roll these questions into one, has the principle of synchronization really affected you in your relationship with God?

If not—if your heart never seems to beat his rhythm—your discipleship is lacking a necessary dimension. It doesn't matter how much you study his Word and gain understanding from it, or even how much of his Word you apply to your daily life. Two out of three aspects of discipleship isn't enough, especially when those two don't connect you to the depths of his heart. You're missing the third element, the key to a sense of fullness in his Spirit. If you feel as empty as many Christians do, you're not feeling the way God feels.

Let's put this in really specific terms. John writes in one of his letters that our loves reveal a lot about our relationship with God. We should love one another because God loved us, because that's what he does. God is love. "If we love one another, God lives in us and his love is made complete in us. . . . Whoever lives in love lives in God, and God in him" (1 John 4:12, 16, NIV). This is the law of synchronization in action, and it applies not only to our relationships with him and other people but also to the systems of this world. "Do not love the world or the things in the world. If anyone loves the world, the love of the Father is not in him" (1 John 2:15). John is able to write these truths because he knows about synchronization: Time spent together in a loving relationship produces a bond in which each person takes on the desires and concerns of the other.

That means that if God loves one of our enemies and we don't, there's still some substantial distance between us. Our hearts haven't connected on that point. If his fervent dream is for his Kingdom to come on earth as it is in heaven, and we aren't really showing much concern for that dream, our emotions don't align with his.

The same dynamic applies to his other emotions—anger, for example. It's no surprise when any one of us feels angry, but to be angry "in the Spirit"? We don't expect that. Neither did Ezekiel, apparently, when the Spirit lifted him up in a vision and took him away: "and I went in bitterness in the heat of my spirit, the hand of the Lord being strong upon me" (Ezekiel 3:14).[11] Here we have an example of the Lord's anger being imparted to a human being, proving that sometimes our anger is legitimate. Our anger is often misplaced and self-centered, which is why Paul and other New Testament writers could group it among the sinful ways of the flesh. But when our anger lines up with God's, it's true and even necessary.

Over and over again in Scripture we see God aligning our hearts with his. He turns our mourning into dancing,[12] he tells us to "fear not" more times than we can count, he offers us his peace in exchange for our anxiety,[13] and he repeatedly urges us to come into his presence with gladness and shouting and loud music and gratitude and an overwhelming sense of exuberance. Why? Because that's his attitude. That's the room temperature of heaven. And this is how our hearts align with his.

TWO KINGS IN CONTRAST

Perhaps the best biblical case study in the pros and cons of emotional living is a comparison between Saul and David. Saul was chosen as Israel's king because the people insisted—through deep but skewed sentiment—that they have a king like other nations around them. So God gave them Saul, whose name meant "asked," as in "you asked for it." And his personality really did reflect the volatile feelings of the masses. Saul was impetuous and brash. At first he served the country well, and later he served his own self-interests. When Goliath taunted Israel's army, Saul seemed resigned to his own humiliation.[14] When he wanted to go into battle and the priest hadn't shown up yet, he impatiently chose to violate divine protocol by performing his own sacrifices.[15] When a sense of vengeance overcame him, he rashly made a vow that could result in the death of his son, and he fully intended to follow through on it.[16] His depressing and angry moods often needed music to soothe them, and even then they couldn't always be helped. A sense of paranoia—part mind tricks and part emotional dysfunction—plagued him, often sending him into a violent rage against David.[17] He eventually seemed to lose his sanity completely. Unredeemed, unaligned emotions led to his downfall.

David, on the other hand, had more constructive emotions—not more pleasant, not more manageable, but more aligned with God's. When God chose David to replace Saul as king, he reminded Samuel the priest that he looks at the heart, not the outward appearance.[18] According to one of Paul's addresses to a Jewish congregation, David was "a man after [God's] own heart" (Acts 13:22, NIV). David apparently had a heart for obedience, which greatly distinguished him from his predecessor. He danced wildly in a worship celebration, he bonded deeply with Saul's son Jonathan, he knew when to be angry and when to lament his losses, he wept openly over his own sin, and he had an enormous capacity to love God and his people. Along with portions of the prophets, his psalms are the most candidly emotive portions of Scripture.

Some people would look at Saul's life and say, "See, you can't be led by your emotions." And that's exactly right—when your emotions are not aligned with God's. It's just as easy, however, to look at David's life and say, "See, godly emotions will make you the kind of person God wants you to be." The difference isn't a matter of feelings versus reason, but of right feelings versus wrong feelings. Saul's twisted, misplaced emotions resulted in a disastrous life. More than any other king in Scripture (or even in world history), David's powerful but bendable emotions drew him close to God and resulted in eternal promises and blessings.

THE HEART OF A PROPHET

God speaks to his people in a multitude of ways, and most of them involve some sort of incarnation. In other words, we don't normally get revelation handed down to us on golden tablets or through a thundering voice from heaven. Human agency is almost always the medium, and even that requires the intense involvement of the individual agent. The idea of an oracle coming through a detached third person—as with a clairvoyant, fortune-teller, or channeler—is foreign to Judeo-Christian history. When God inspired the writers of the Bible, they became a part of the story. He used their personalities, experiences, and emotions to tell his story. They were not passive observers of divine truth.

We see that most clearly in the prophets. Jeremiah didn't have the privilege of just telling the Israelites how bad God's judgment would be. He had to live through it—to experience the anger of God and the heartache of betrayal, to suffer the persecution of godliness and the crushing weight of wrath—to represent God's heart to people and people's hearts to God. He is known as the weeping prophet because he shed genuine tears and lived a tragic life—all to demonstrate the perspectives of God.

Hosea did too, though in a less tumultuous time than Jeremiah. This prophet had to marry a prostitute in order to portray God's feelings about Israel's unfaithfulness. God was no dispassionate deity who would casually pour out his wrath on disobedience; he was a grieving husband whose heart was torn apart by a bride who gave sexual favors to practically any man she met. Hosea didn't pass that information along as a memo. He lived it—every tearful, jealous, frustrating, painful moment of it. Why? Because God shares his heart with his people.

Every prophet experienced the heart of God beating within them, but they weren't the only ones. We mentioned David above; read the psalms slowly sometime and notice how profusely his feelings spill onto each page. Every extreme is there, from the pits of despair to the heights of ecstasy, from the outrage of injustice to the compassion of extravagant grace, from the awe of majesty to the dancing of deliverance. Not all of the emotions in there came from God, but if David poured out something inconsistent with the divine heart, you usually see a shift before the end of the psalm. These passages are case studies in emotional transformation. If you have an emotion that isn't in David's psalms, you may not be human. And if you have one that can't be brought in line with God's heart, you may not be willing.

Not surprisingly, there's profound wisdom in God's methods. He didn't give us his Word as a list of principles and regulations, as a how-to book on the right way to live, or as a systematic theology. He gave us the human experience of the divine, and the divine experience of the human. His mind, his will, and his emotions intersect with real lives in real history, and the result is an experience of his character at a depth that theology can never reach.

I've always been amused at people who say you can't base your doctrine on experience, even though all biblical doctrine is based on somebody's experience. We get foundational principles of faith from some pretty strange experiences of a man named Abraham. We build key doctrines of God's saving grace on the testimony of people who said God opened up a sea to deliver them and a river to give them their own land. We understand the sacrificial system because an octogenarian heard thunder and saw fire on a mountaintop. We trace our spiritual empowerment back to a room where people saw something like tongues of fire and started babbling in other languages. And much of Christian doctrine comes through a man who says he saw a resurrected Savior on a road in the desert—even though his traveling companions didn't see a thing.[19] The same guy later wrote that he had gotten a lot of his revelation during an apparent out-of-body experience in paradise.[20] All biblical doctrine comes directly or indirectly from someone's experience with God.

God's mind, his will, and his emotions intersect with real lives in real history, and the result is an experience of his character at a depth that theology can never reach.

The same dynamic also goes for emotions. We hear, "You should never base doctrine on your feelings," yet the Bible is filled with theological statements that come directly from the deep, inspired emotions of prophets, priests, kings, and common people like you and me. The irony is that the people who are most vocal about biblical authority are the ones who most loudly reject the means by which biblical authority came to us: through subjective experiences, emotions, and impressions. Their warnings about adding to Scripture are entirely right; we don't want to create any new doctrine because the canon is now closed and the Word is sufficient. But God still communicates the way he did centuries ago when Jeremiah, Hosea, and David were writing about the inspired emotions that welled up within them.

I'm certainly not recommending that we live in any way contrary to Scripture or that we revise any part of the Word as we have it. But we still need God's guidance about where to live, what kind of ministry to be involved in, how to apply our spiritual gifts in specific situations, who to partner with in marriage or business, and so on. And not all of that guidance is going to come from objective observations of the voice of God. Much of it will be inner impressions, spiritual impulses, and other intangible, faith-stretching means. If the prophets and the king after God's own heart are any example, gut feelings will often be a substantial part of the guidance.

That's how God works with his people. It's up close and personal, not a performance of principles. There's nothing formulaic or automatic about it. The way he spoke last time may not be the way he speaks this time—or then again, it may be. His desire for us is dynamic and decidedly intimate. We can't get by on any other kind of relationship.

FEELING HIS PULSE

Whenever you feel something—anything, especially related to a relationship issue—think about how your emotions might reflect God's heart. I've touched on this already, but it's worth some elaboration because this practice has the potential to radically transform your relationship with God. Even when your feelings are the product of mistakes or misperceptions, there's probably something in them to connect you with God.

For example, the Bible frequently compares our relationship with God to a child-parent relationship. The feelings you have toward your own children may give you a pretty good idea of how God feels about you—or, if your experience is a negative example, of how God *doesn't* feel about you. If you're overwhelmed with love for your children and know that the Bible says God is love, you've gotten a powerful glimpse into his heart. Or if you are frustrated and impatient with your children, and you know the Bible speaks of God's discipline, you can understand to some degree the attitudes behind his corrections. You might also marvel at the contrast between us and him—how patient and enduring he is in spite of our childish rebellion. Your feelings don't need to match his exactly in order to reveal truth to you. They can even be the opposite of his. Either way, you're sharing an experience with him—parenting—and learning about the dynamics of love, patience, and correction, and how his Fatherhood either parallels or goes way beyond our own.

In a romantic relationship, the dynamics are different, but they're equally relevant. From all the wedding terminology in the Bible relating to God and his people—the Song of Solomon as an allegory, the Bridegroom and the bride, the wedding described at the end of Revelation—we can begin to understand the depths and power of relentless love. We get glimpses of his jealousy in our own jealousy, of the intensity of his love in our own love, of the ways in which he bonds with us in the way we bond with others, and so on. The power of love is never more visible than in a passionate romance; that kind of relationship can be very descriptive of God's pursuit of intimacy with his people.

There are many other ways to apply this. If you've ever poured your effort into a gift for someone who then treated it carelessly and casually, you have a hint of God's sentiments when we disrespect creation or take for granted the carefully prepared blessings he's given us. If you've ever been offended by someone who misrepresented you to others, you have a fraction of a picture of how God reacts to the devil's and the world's many slanders against him. If you know a wonderful person who has low self-esteem, your sadness over his or her false identity correlates pretty well with God's sadness over us. Or if, in the midst of a philosophical discussion about the mysteries of the universe, you realize that a real Person is not only at the center of them but also listening attentively to every word, your voice might grow more sensitive and your points less strident.

When we start to think and feel this way, we multiply our connections with God and sense his closeness. But more than that, we find that God actually begins to communicate with us through our emotional responses to events and people. We will hear his voice saying, "You know how you treasure that friendship? That's how I treasure my friendship with you." Or, "The pleasure you feel when someone compliments your work is the kind of pleasure I feel when my people praise me." Not only have we trained our perceptions to sense his voice, we've also cultivated an intimate relationship in which hearts are knit together and secrets are shared.[21]

If you're wondering whether this kind of heart interaction with God is biblical, look at the prophet Jonah. After he has preached to Nineveh about God's coming judgment and the godless city has repented, Jonah gets angry that God has spared them. He is not feeling the emotions of God by any stretch of the imagination. Far from reflecting God's mercy, he instead is fixated on judgment and pride. So how does God synchronize the heart of his servant (and the readers observing this story) with his own pulse? He grows a vine for shade, which causes Jonah to rejoice, and then takes the vine away, which makes Jonah angry. Then God brings his lesson home: "You pity the plant, for which you did not labor, nor did you make it grow. . . . Should not I pity Nineveh, that great city?"[22] God speaks to his prophet through the prophet's own emotions by relating those feelings to divine sympathies. The heart of the Father for a lost people is made clear.

That's exactly how God sometimes speaks to us to synchronize our hearts with his. A life situation will suddenly shed light on God's relationship with his people, and we'll understand a bit more about who he is and how he feels. The more we notice our emotional dynamics, the more we're able to compare or contrast them with the emotions attributed to God in Scripture—and the more we share his experiences and bond with him.

THE UNEXPECTED COMMANDMENTS

When friends or family members express their feelings of sadness or anger, many of us will offer a word of encouragement to let them know that those feelings are normal. "That's okay," we tell them. "You're allowed to be angry" (or sad or whatever other emotion). And while that's true, biblically speaking, it's also a major understatement. We're not only allowed to experience those feelings, we're instructed to. It's part of our discipleship; this is how we get to know God. And this instruction doesn't only apply to the negative feelings we think we shouldn't have; it's also true for the positive emotions of joy and celebration. Scripture gives us numerous commands on how to feel: Rejoice in the Lord; serve the Lord with gladness; fear not; be strong and courageous; be anxious for nothing. God is intensely interested in our ability to conform to his heart.

Our need for emotional transformation comes with abundant promises. Every "fear not" in the Bible is a call to conform to the emotions of heaven. God turns our mourning into dancing and gives us beauty for ashes. He invites us to enter into the joy of our Master and to look forward to the day when every tear is wiped away. We're called to leap for joy when we are persecuted and to rejoice that our names are written in heaven. He delights over us with singing and invites us to delight in him. When he delivers his people, there's a celebration. When he forgives sinners, there's much gladness in heaven. And we are welcomed into that emotional environment at any time and to whatever extent we'll accept it.

Remember the older brother in the story of the prodigal son? When the younger son returns, the father runs to him, welcomes him home, and plans a huge party. The older brother is resentful and angry that no one has ever celebrated *him*. Clearly, his heart is not in sync with his father's. The father points out that he would have allowed this son to have a party at any time; "all that is mine is yours" (Luke 15:31). But the elder brother had always been too busy with his sense of obligation and his serious devotion to his father's business to do something as frivolous as enjoy the father's blessings. Now the father wants to celebrate a restored relationship—and he wants the older son to share his heart. This son, like us, has *always* been invited to know his father's joy. But, also like us, he hasn't noticed his opportunity to do that.

The implications are enormous. In any situation in which you're consciously following the Lord, ask yourself this critical question: *Am I feeling the same way God feels about this situation?* Understanding his instructions is certainly relevant, and obeying them is essential. But to do either or both without the divine heart beating within you is not going to help you grow or bear much fruit. Discipleship that's emotionally disconnected from God is an empty discipleship, and while it's better than nothing, it isn't going to please either you or him in the long run. Like the prodigal's older brother, you could have had a party anytime you wanted to. You could have grieved with your father when the son went away, and you could have celebrated when he returned. If you don't, you have chosen religion over relationship, and God grieves over you as much as he grieves for a prodigal.

Next time you hear of a miracle, of a sinner repenting, of widows and orphans in distress, of an attack of the enemy, or of an exuberant worship service, take the temperature of both your heart and the climate of heaven. If there's a discrepancy, never rationalize it. Instead, pursue a transformation by asking God to give you his pulse.

CHAPTER 9

a fellowship of three equals

how the mind, will, and emotions work together

IN A GAME against the Boston Bruins in March 1955, Montreal Canadiens player Maurice Richard was greatly offended when a Bruin's hockey stick hit him in the head. Though a penalty was about to be called, Richard took a vengeance-is-mine approach and whacked the offender in the face repeatedly with his stick. In the ensuing melee, Richard punched a referee in the face twice, knocking him unconscious.

It was Richard's second attack on an official that year, and the league suspended him for the rest of the season. Canadiens fans thought that penalty was much too severe and were outraged. Four days later, with Montreal still in an uproar, the Canadiens played the Detroit Red Wings on home ice, and league president Clarence Campbell attended with his fiancée. Protesters were rather demonstrative in their anger; every time the Red Wings scored, the home crowd threw vegetables and eggs at Campbell and his future bride. The pelting stopped only after tear gas was released. The arena was evacuated and the game was forfeited, but that didn't end the chaos. A riot broke out in the streets of Montreal and resulted in hundreds of thousands of dollars worth of property damage to the neighborhood and injury to nearly forty people.

If you were to survey several people about the cause of the riot, you would probably get a variety of answers. Some people would point to the behavior of Richard and of the debris-tossing Montreal crowd, or even of the security forces that employed tear gas. Any of those actions could be seen as provoking the riot.

Other people would fault all the misperceptions involved. In fact, that's exactly what some observers did. The Canadiens' general manager blamed the media for magnifying a hockey player's popularity in the first place and turning him into an idol; and some social scientists blamed the political and economic alienation felt by many Quebecois who let an irrelevant hockey war serve as a catalyst event for protest.

Then, of course, there are those who would simply say that emotions got out of control—that in spite of circumstances and offenses, hostilities should never have risen to that level among civilized people. Sports fans ought to have more self-discipline than to vent their anger by hurling produce at an adversary and trashing the streets of their city.

Among all of these explanations of the riot, which one is right? Was misbehavior the culprit? Was the riot the result of misunderstanding? Or was it a matter of misplaced passions gone wild?

This is a trick question, of course. You know as well as I do that all three conspired together to create the kind of chaos every stable society dreads. None of them alone would have resulted in a riot. Passion by itself doesn't accomplish anything unless the mind and the behavior submit to it. Likewise, the behavior itself would have been irrelevant and meaningless (and easily stopped) if thoughts and passions hadn't contributed to it. And perceptions wouldn't have been enough to cause a riot if those perceptions evoked no emotional response or required no action. No element of our personalities alone disrupts the peace of a kingdom unless the other two cooperate. Our mind, will, and emotions function as a single triune entity.

THE "SOUL" OF GOD

The Bible speaks of God's mind, his will, and his emotions. When it says "he does all that he pleases" (Psalm 115:3), it invokes two of those aspects of his being: the will and the emotions. When, in a discussion about like-mindedness, Paul wrote that it's God who is at work in us "both to will and to work for his good pleasure" (Philippians 2:13), he tied all three aspects together. When God put Moses in the cleft of a rock and let his glory pass by, he revealed himself as merciful, gracious, slow to anger, abounding in steadfast love and faithfulness (*truth*, in some translations), and treating his people with both forgiveness and judgment.[1] This recipe combines all three: his mind (truth), his will (his treatment of his people), and his emotions (love, mercy, anger, etc.)—heavy on the emotions. Ample scriptural evidence portrays God as fully integrated and balanced in his personality, with each aspect related to the others.

If the basis of our personalities is the image of God, then this integrity and balance applies to us. Discipleship that emphasizes one aspect more than another is not a clear depiction of godliness. The question we need to focus on, then, is how to proceed with the elements of our soul united. And the best way to do that is to see how our biblical heroes did it.

Models of Integrity

Let's start with the father of faith: Abraham. At various stages of his life, all three elements got him into trouble; and at later stages, all three elements fulfilled God's purposes for him.

His reasoning compelled him to lie about his wife, Sarah, on two occasions, telling rivals that she was his sister so he wouldn't be killed. The result, however, was that she was almost incorporated into royal harems, where she would have faded into biblical oblivion and missed having the son of a promise in her old age. Abraham's reasoning did not serve him well on those occasions.

Neither did it serve him well when he listened to his wife's logical plan for him to father a child through her maidservant, Hagar. The result was Ishmael, whose natural descendents have been a constant source of conflict for the chosen people for thousands of years. The rationalism of a patriarch was clearly not a good foundation for faith.

But neither was his will, which fully cooperated with his intellect in both circumstances, ungallantly risking his wife's purity in his rivals' harems and producing Ishmael through Hagar. Reason is powerless if actions won't follow its lead, and Abraham gave his thought processes plenty of power.

If we look to Abraham's emotions for true faith, we will again be disappointed. He got rather impatient with God's plan, lamenting his childlessness before the Almighty as if to say, "I know you promised a son, but I'm not feeling very confident about that. In fact, I'm sad, desperate, and lonely."[2] No, if Abraham's feelings reigned, he might never have become the father of faith.

But in his instances of spiritual maturity, we see all three working together. First, his mind surely didn't understand the long delay in God's promise to give him a son, but Romans 4 indicates that he was "fully convinced" that God would keep his word. The mind accepted the promise of God without having to prove it first. And he couldn't have understood the test of taking Isaac, "the son of laughter," up on a mountain to sacrifice him, but Hebrews says his reason complied with God's instructions: "He considered that God was able even to raise him from the dead" (Hebrews 11:19). A mind conformed to the character of God is elevated to take hold of things it can't explain. Abraham's mind embraced truth and acknowledged God when his reason couldn't necessarily sort it all out.

Abraham's willful obedience was remarkably clear. He left Haran without knowing where he was going—a clear triumph for the will over the mind. And in addition to not understanding why he was sacrificing Isaac, he certainly must not have felt like doing it—yet he proceeded up the mountain. We could conclude from his example that obedience clearly trumps understanding and emotion, but the overall testimony of his life indicates that even when he didn't understand the specifics of God's plan, he understood the nature of God. Furthermore, even when he didn't feel like obeying, he wanted God to be his great reward.[3] Just as Jesus went to the Cross for a future emotion of joy, Abraham was willing to sacrifice Isaac for the joy of knowing God. As the chapter of faith testifies, "If they had been *thinking* [mind] of that land from which they had gone out, they would have had opportunity [or the will] to return. But as it is, they *desire* [emotions] a better country, that is, a heavenly one" (Hebrews 11:15-16, italics added).

That's one way Abraham's emotions fit together with his understanding and his will to produce faith. Desire is a powerful fuel for the soul. The fact that Abraham was willing to sacrifice "the son of laughter" is not a statement of his suppression of joyful feelings, but rather a statement that a greater joy comes through obeying. When Abraham lamented earlier about his childlessness, it was immediately after God had told him, "I am . . . your very great reward" (Genesis 15:1, NIV). It may have taken a while to sink in, but by the sacrifice of Isaac, it was clear that "God the reward" had become more pleasant and satisfying to Abraham than "Isaac the reward." This wasn't a denial of one joy; it was a choice between two.

Desire is a powerful fuel for the soul.

As you can see, sorting out the mental, willful, and emotional elements of Abraham's faith is virtually impossible. One fueled another, which in turn influenced another, which led back to the first. They all danced together to respond to the personality of God, because the personality of God is an integrated union of them all.

We've already looked extensively at David's emotional response to Goliath, but we can easily see that emotions weren't the only part of his personality to kick in that day. Obedience resulted from those emotions, and both were nourished by an understanding that God's glory is paramount and that he defends those who battle for his reputation. Trying to figure out which comes first becomes a chicken-and-egg kind of mystery.

It's obvious from other episodes in David's life what happens when the three elements get out of balance. In the Bathsheba fiasco,[4] emotions and actions clearly dominated reason, and the results were tragic. That doesn't prove that understanding should guide our emotions and actions, because the Goliath episode would never have happened if that were the case. Fighting Goliath was completely illogical, but it was the right thing to do and the only way to satisfy David's zeal. But when he saw Bathsheba and desired her, his zeal did not need to be satisfied and his willfulness needed to be put in restraints.

The mind/will/emotions conundrum can't be formulized, as proven by David's life. On one occasion, he needed to follow his heart. On another, his heart was desperately wicked. If we take either example and make a principle out of it, we'll end up missing the heart of God quite often. David acted on his passions against Goliath, restrained his passions when he had opportunities to kill Saul, and acted on his passions with Bathsheba. Sometimes his heart was right and he knew it; sometimes it was wrong and he knew it; and sometimes it was wrong and he didn't know it. It's hard to make a pattern out of that.

If we say it's wrong to act out of our emotions and base our relationship with God on desires, we eliminate from the Bible not only David's unlikely victory, but also the example of Hannah.[5] Her desire for a child was in large part based on envy and despair, though she was also willing to let God in on the fruits of her promise. And if we say it's wrong not to follow our hearts, we eliminate the example of Esther, who, out of compassion and grief for her people, risked her life to enter the king's presence even though she clearly wasn't convinced it would work. And if we say that understanding is meant to guide both the will and the heart, we eliminate every radical act based on supernatural guidance, like Abraham's sacrifice of Isaac, Hosea's marriage to a prostitute, Mary's belief that the Holy Spirit would impregnate her, and every one of Jesus' miracles. Any time we elevate one of the soul's elements over the others, we can find a clear rebuke in Scripture.

A balanced understanding of our personalities will lead us to two important conclusions: (1) when unredeemed, every aspect of our souls is dangerous; and (2) when redeemed, any one of them is capable of rising up in the strength of the Spirit and grabbing hold of God. None of them should be elected dictator by the other two, and none should try to beat the others into submission. That won't make us more Christlike. Unless we hold all three in balance, we do violence to the image within us.

DISCERNMENT

At this point, we should be desperately hungry for discernment. If God's will is sometimes completely illogical to the human mind— even a mind saturated with scriptural truth—we can't always count on our reason. If his will is sometimes completely contrary to the deepest feelings of our hearts—even hearts that love the Lord—we can't count on our emotions either. And if his will is sometimes diametrically opposed to our own—even a will that's well-trained in submission—then we can't even count on raw obedience to get us to accomplish his purposes. Any of the three can be deceived at any time. So how do we know what to think, feel, and do?

If the Bible had come to us as a set of propositional truths—principles and theological explanations—this would be a good spot to lay it out. But that's not how God has revealed himself. He absolutely refuses to give us formulas for living because we'd gravitate to the formulas and miss the relationship he desires. So our method for discernment isn't going to be spelled out for us. It can't be. It comes from communion with his Spirit. The only way to get it is to pursue intimacy with him.

That said, we can look for a few clues—not hard-and-fast principles, but general guidelines—in Scripture to help us sort out the interplay between the mind, the will, and the emotions:

- *Don't let any element of your personality consistently rule the others.* When actions habitually defy the mind and heart, the result is hypocrisy. When the mind habitually usurps the will and the heart, the result is skepticism and doubt. When the heart habitually rises above the will and the mind, the result is emotionalism. What you end up with is a collection of Pharisees (empty obedience), Sadducees (intellectual pride), or zealots (emotional vigilantes), none of which was well-tolerated by Jesus. Each dimension of your soul can lead at appropriate times, but none should lead as a practice.

- *Don't let any element of your personality atrophy.* When actions are paralyzed, the result is disobedience, either by commission or omission. When the understanding is paralyzed, the result is deception. When emotions are paralyzed, the result is apathy. What you end up with is a church or lifestyle that is busy, gullible, or static, all of which Jesus warned us against.

- *When one dimension of your personality is sending you red flags, don't overrule it until you've gotten confirmation from God to do so.* The prophet Jonah had a lot of reservations—intellectual and emotional—about going to Nineveh to preach repentance, and it's clear that he should have simply obeyed without understanding or feeling like it. But much of the book focuses on the understanding he gained in the belly of a fish (he "remembered the LORD" and came to his senses[6]) and on the heart attitude of God revealed through an illustration of a withered vine. The book concludes with a heart statement by God: "Should not I pity Nineveh, that great city?" (Jonah 4:11). God's concern for those who didn't know their right hand from their left, spiritually speaking, is the primary message of the story.

I'm pretty sure if Jonah had asked God for his heart of compassion up front, that embarrassing fish-belly incident never would have been necessary. The mind, will, and emotions of the prophet could have synced with God's Spirit beforehand. The red flags Jonah felt emotionally when he received his calling to Nineveh could have driven him to God rather than sent him in the opposite direction of obedience. And in that holy presence, he would have received clarification and reassurance about his mission. Just as our doubts should drive us to God to learn his thoughts, our emotional reservations should drive us to him to absorb his feelings.

• *Test fleeting impulses.* King Saul acted rashly on numerous occasions, letting his emotions rule his more stable faculties. When emotions are godly, that's not necessarily a problem from time to time. But Saul's feelings weren't very consistent with God's, and they often resulted in disaster. One notable example was that rash statement we looked at earlier, the vow he made when the Philistines had gotten on his last nerve: "Cursed be the man who eats food until it is evening and I am avenged on my enemies" (1 Samuel 14:24). If Saul had thought that statement through, he might have realized that a fast during battle might weaken his army and that a good man who wasn't aware of the curse might unwittingly eat some food. As it turns out, the good man who ended up doing that was his son Jonathan. Saul was prepared to follow through on his vow by killing his own son; Jonathan was spared only by popular demand.[7]

Just as our doubts should drive us to God to learn his thoughts, our emotional reservations should drive us to him to absorb his feelings.

It's possible to overreact to new information or have a sudden emotional response to a set of circumstances, and the results in each case can be tragic. Just as impulsive behavior disqualified Saul from his kingship, it sabotaged Samson's power and usefulness and eventually resulted in his death. God's Spirit may inspire you and move you through your emotions, but rarely, if ever, does he insist on an immediate, unquestioning reaction. His inspiration is consistent, deep, and lasting—and he supports those who will test it to make sure it's his. If it's enduring, consistent with his character and his plans, and growing stronger during genuine worship and prayer, it probably is.

- *If you feel empty for very long, something's wrong.* Solomon's emptiness as recorded in Ecclesiastes was clearly a symptom of misperceptions, disobedience, and alienation from the heart of God. Though there's wisdom in that sermon, the book is most useful for its assessment of life without the Spirit. The hopelessness and despair throbbing from its pages are confirmation that Solomon really didn't finish well. His indiscriminate marriages and his foolish idolatry negated the practical benefits of his earlier wisdom. He's an example of someone who had all the right understanding but whose heart was inconsistent with God's. His mind and his will didn't suffice. He needed to connect with his Lord and embrace the emotional side of discipleship. Whenever we linger long in a joyless or apathetic season, our immediate reaction should be to run to God and ask for a deeper connection with him.

- *Never forget the special connection between the heart and the Spirit.* Just as he did with many of his most faithful servants, God will lead you in ways that transcend your understanding and offend your will. I've already mentioned some of the most noteworthy case studies such as Abraham, Hosea, and Jeremiah. Add to that list Noah, Ezekiel, Isaiah, Paul at his conversion, and many others, and you begin to understand Pascal's quote about the heart having its reasons that reason doesn't understand. Seriously, how would you react if God told you to spend decades building an ark under blue skies for a flood yet to come? Or to walk around naked for three years to prove a point?[8] Or to cook your food over dung during the 390 days you're lying on one side in public in order to represent God's disfavor?[9] If you're relying on the understanding and active side of your soul, you'll miss God's instructions. The voice of God came through subjective experience to these people because they were in tune with his heart.

EXERCISES FOR THE SOUL

People who say "I feel that God spoke to me about . . ." draw a lot of criticism from legalistic and intellectual Christians. The common response is, "It doesn't matter what you *feel*—God will only speak to you through his Word." Then the critic goes on to discuss the importance of raw obedience even when understanding and emotion are absent or contradictory.

The reason for this reaction, of course, is that we all know people who have abused or misrepresented the "God told me" line. Personal revelation attracts the same suspicion that emotions do because both are subjective and both can lead us astray. I won't rehash my contention here that the mind and the will can lead us astray just as easily because we've already covered that. But there's a valid concern in these warnings against "feeling" God's voice.

Rejecting such a claim outright, however, is unwarranted. The Bible usually doesn't describe in detail how the prophets heard God's voice; it just tells us that they did. I suspect that sometimes the voice was audible, other times it was visual, and most of the time it was "sensed" in the Spirit by receptive people and confirmed in other ways. We can't be dogmatic about the heart language God used with them. But having perceived his voice myself—as many Christians have, including the above critics who likely "felt" called to ministry at one point in their lives—I've learned some ways to cultivate my sensitivity to it. Through spiritual "exercise," we can strengthen each aspect of our personalities to interact with the Spirit more clearly and function in a more balanced fashion.

You're probably already familiar with the first two practices, so I won't expend many words on them. They are the two primary principles of discipleship that we've long emphasized above emotional responses to God.

- *Read the Word.* The mind is fueled by understanding biblical truth. It's an information processor, so we need to feed it information. That's its diet. This involves ample time reading the Bible itself, but also time listening to others' insights through sermons, books, and formal education. The classic supporting verse is 2 Timothy 2:15: "Do your best to present yourself to God as one approved, a worker who has no need to be ashamed, rightly handling the word of truth."

- *Apply the Word.* This is where most modern discipleship advice ends. It's the ultimate goal, according to many. And it's true that unapplied knowledge is pointless. As Jesus asked, "Why do you call me 'Lord, Lord,' and do not do what I say?" (Luke 6:46, NIV). It's a convicting question, isn't it? Those who know God's Word are compelled to live God's Word. Otherwise their faith is lifeless. The classic supporting verses for this discipline say so explicitly: "Be doers of the word, and not hearers only, deceiving yourselves. . . . Faith by itself, if it does not have works, is dead" (James 1:22; 2:17).

- *Feel the Word.* The evangelical community typically backs off and says, "Feelings come and go." But the same teachers who warn against feelings also talk about the difference between head knowledge and heart knowledge, and how only one of those really impacts your life. They've correctly assessed the situation, but offer little advice on what to do about it. How does truth move from your head to your heart? And is that even always the right direction?

I believe that frequently God's truth is meant to enter the heart and then influence the head. I know that sounds like heresy to many—

or at least like the tendencies of the uneducated—but it's scripturally sound. "With the *heart* one believes and is justified" (Romans 10:10, italics added). "You who were once slaves of sin [behavior] have become obedient *from the heart* [emotions] to the standard of teaching to which you were committed [understanding]" (Romans 6:17, italics added). "The good man out of the good treasure *of his heart* brings forth what is good" (Luke 6:45, italics added). The seat of spiritual truth in the soul of human beings seems to be in the heart.

So how do you build it up? You have to do more than read the Word and apply it. Even meditating on the Word isn't enough, though that's certainly a part of the process. Truth moves into the heart most effectively and efficiently when we interact with the Word—both the Word as Scripture and the Word as Jesus, the living *logos* of John 1:1: "In the beginning was the Word, and the Word was with God, and the Word was God."

The seat of spiritual truth in the soul of human beings seems to be in the heart.

Let me explain what that means. When you study the Bible, listen to a sermon, read a book like this one, fill in the blanks of a discipleship workbook, discuss biblical principles in a small group, or whatever else you do to process information as a Christian, there's a voice in the depths of your heart that wants to interact with you. This voice desires more than a "Wow, great insight!" when you come across a good point, more than an extended time of meditating on the implications of that insight, and even more than a diligent application of what you just learned—though all of those are good. The voice invites you into a real conversation. The Spirit that promised to flow out of your innermost being like rivers of living water has opinions and advice and a desire for intimacy. You can pretty well assume that when you've turned your heart over to him, asked him to guard your heart and mind as you converse with him, and submitted yourself to the images, impressions, and promptings that rise up within you, you're hearing that voice. This is the time to talk and to listen—to feel the warm breath of intimacy on your face and to incline your ear to the deep secrets of eternity. This is where a relationship flourishes.

Mystical? Yes, absolutely. Unapologetically. And that's what makes solid, wise disciples nervous. It's too subjective for most tastes, and it seems so open to deception. But what this really boils down to is trust—which, in itself, is a heart issue with God. Communion with him requires an emotional investment that plows the ground of your heart to receive his affections. In that place of deep intimacy, he shares his heart and speaks.

Look at it this way: Do you place more faith in your ability to be deceived or in his ability to keep you from deception? Because if you're constantly guarding against any deceptive feelings in your communion with him, and if you're adamantly opposed to "feeling" like he said something to you, you're basically refusing to believe his promise that he will keep you safe from the enemy's wiles. Jesus said, "My sheep hear my voice, and I know them, and they follow me. . . . no one will snatch them out of my hand" (John 10:27-28). It's true that the old heart can be full of deception, but the new, redeemed heart can synchronize with God. You have to decide which is greater: the weakness of your heart or the power and love of his Spirit. And while he never asks you to be undiscerning, he does ask you to trust him. The relationship can't progress unless you do.

Pardon the graphic illustration, but our fear of deception is a lot like refusing to climb into bed with a spouse whom we think might only be feigning love for us. Will he or she listen to our sweet secrets and turn them against us in the morning? This romantic experience won't be very romantic if we anticipate a betrayal of trust. That kind of relationship results in alienation and disillusionment. That's *not* the kind of relationship God would even consider having with us.

To pay attention to the deep movements of our spirit—all those intuitive impressions that occur during a conversation with God— requires a lot of trust, but he has assured us that he's trustworthy. When we sense repeated thoughts and feelings that are birthed out of communion with him, it's a faithless slander of his character to analyze those thoughts and feelings to death and rationalize that they were too subjective to be his voice. If my wife says, "I love you," it would be extremely insulting to obsess all day about whether she really meant it and whether she really said it or I was just hearing what I wanted to hear. God put his Spirit within us to speak and to enjoy our fellowship. If we're not hearing and communing in a very real way, something is seriously wrong.

So what are you hearing? Are you so "discerning" that nothing God says to you can qualify as his authentic voice? Or are you listening with a trusting heart? Are the emotions you feel coming from your times of communion with him? And if you've asked for that, can you trust that he answered?

This is where discipleship becomes real. This is where abundant life becomes more than a promise that must be true even though we can't feel it. This is where God speaks to prophets and radically transforms the hearts of his servants. This is where we can experience the feelings of God.

CHAPTER 10

an open door to God's heart

knowing his joy, bearing his fruit

AS I WRITE THIS, I'm sitting on a beach watching my son play in the water. I tried to finish this book before the family vacation began, but this chapter didn't quite come together in time. So today I'm enjoying the breeze, taking some notes, and realizing that what I'm observing makes a perfect illustration to launch into the topic of God's pleasure in sharing his feelings.

My son Timothy is not quite as adventurous in the water as other eight-year-olds yet, partly because we haven't been to the beach for over two years and he has to get used to waves again. He began this day almost afraid to stick a toe in the waves, and when he got blindsided by a wall of seawater at one point, I thought he might give up the ocean for good. But now that he's gotten rid of the taste and the sting, he's bravely challenging the sea. Each wave gets a karate chop as it barrels past him, and some of them are even getting kicked. That's because a few minutes ago, a boy he just met let him borrow a boogie board, and Timothy has had the pleasure of riding some waves into the shore. No casual observer would notice the significance of this feat, but for Timothy it's a substantial triumph. The waves have been conquered, and now they are worthy only of getting karate-chopped by the Atlantic's newest wave warrior. My son is having a great time.

Dads get a lot of pleasure watching their children enjoy life. There's something deeply satisfying in seeing someone you love have fun, win victories, and ride the waves. It's even satisfying to watch them feel the sting of a cold slap of saltwater, not because you wish discomfort on your kids, but because you remember the first time you were so rudely treated by the sea. Such necessary rites of passage link your children's experiences with yours, and this opportunity for you to comfort them and sympathize with them may someday even become one of their most cherished memories—because you shared an experience and the feelings that went with it. Both the challenges and the joys warm the heart of a dad who loves his son.

Just as I enjoyed Timothy's romp in the waves, God enjoys watching us delight in his gifts and experience his feelings. His pleasure in connecting with us not only applies to the serious things of life—his mission becoming our mission, for example, or his values becoming our values—but also in the simple playfulness of creation. God looked at the work of his hands and called it "good" and "very good," and he's delighted when we see it the same way. He made peacocks to strut, dolphins to frolic, llamas to spit, fireflies to glow, penguins to waddle, parrots to mock, dogs to chase their own tails, and hyenas to laugh—not because these various activities are essential to survival, but because the variety is intriguing and sometimes humorous.

Not only does God enjoy our warm hearts and delighted smiles, he shares his deepest feelings and gravest concerns with us. When he confided to Abraham his plans to destroy Sodom and Gomorrah, the result wasn't only Abraham's intercession for those cities. Rather, the intercession sprang out of a mutual sense of tragedy and resulted in a joint lamentation over the fact that not even ten righteous people could be found there.[1] Abraham and the Lord were of one mind at that moment. At times the Lord of hosts calls us to weep and wail for the calamities we have brought upon ourselves.[2] Why? Does he delight in our misery? No, he wants us to see with his eyes, to feel as he feels, to join in the divine sentiments of his heart. There's intimacy in those places just as there's intimacy in joy. God has placed us in a visceral world and given us a visceral gospel so we can know who he is. He invites us to enter in to the deeply personal places he's prepared for us. Let's explore how.

God enjoys watching us delight in his gifts and experience his feelings.

THE HARD EVIDENCE OF LOVE

One of the most undeniable God-given instincts in human nature is a mother's urge to hold and caress her newborn baby. Even evolutionary biologists are sold on the evidence that human touch is necessary not only to keep the child in close proximity to his or her caregivers, but also to stimulate neurological development and to create an emotional template for the child's future relationships. In other words, both the brain and the heart need the affectionate touch of a parent.

Evidence shows that a single heart cell isolated but kept alive will gradually lose its rhythm, fibrillate, and then die. Another isolated heart cell placed on the same microscope slide will also begin the same process, but when the two cells are placed in close proximity, they begin to beat in unison again.[3] It's that law of synchronization in action again, and it's not only desirable, it's necessary for survival. This may be one reason a mother intuitively places her child first at the left breast, where her heart and the baby's commune in closeness. The human heart releases a hormone that dramatically affects every other system of the body.[4] Heart connections are vital for proper growth.

Science is also clear on what happens when human touch is withdrawn from an infant, as well as when genuine love is not well expressed throughout childhood years. Neurological and social development is stunted. Children withdraw and feel isolated, paying for their alienation for the rest of their lives with all sorts of mental, physical, and social ailments. In effect, when the warmth of love is not present in our lives, we wither and die.

The law of synchronization is not only desirable, it's necessary for survival.

This is exactly the spiritual state of people who do not experience an emotional connection with God. Very few Christians see God as someone who will tenderly love and caress us. We are so fearful of his demands that we become isolated from his warmth. We perceive him as the kind of father who, if he were human, would be universally accused of neglect. Because of that false perception, we feel alienated. Our minds, bodies, hearts, and relationships suffer. No matter how hard we try to be obedient to God and to trust in him, we can't. The sinful nature within us is fueled by a lack of emotional fulfillment, and we seek all kinds of substitutes or opiates to relieve the pain. Under those conditions, we can't be who God made us to be.

I think it's safe to say that this breaks his heart. His desire is to enjoy his children and for them to enjoy him. He loves to watch us play in the waves, so to speak, or to see us feel fulfilled to the very core of our being. His heart craves the satisfaction of ours.

We've talked about the harsh strain of Christianity out there that majors on self-denial and criticizes this idea of "fulfillment." We're reminded constantly that God is not a spiritual Santa Claus, that he doesn't exist to make us happy, that our job is obedience whether we like it or not, and that everything in us must be sacrificed to his will. That's all true, of course, but it certainly isn't the whole story. And if we follow it as though it *is* the whole story, we'll wither and die just as surely as a newborn who never gets touched. God invites us into his joy, offers to do more than we can ask or even imagine,[5] promises us abundant life,[6] and fulfills us in his presence.[7] We've got no business emphasizing the sterile, harsh demands of his will and thinking we're his mouthpiece in doing so.

THE HARD MASTER

In the week before his execution, Jesus spoke to his disciples about his return. He said it would be like a man who went on a journey and distributed his possessions among his three servants. To one, he gave five talents (each talent worth more than a thousand dollars), to another he gave two, and to another he gave one. The first two saw this responsibility as a trust issue, invested their master's money, and were able to return to him double its worth. The third buried his talent in fear and returned to the master exactly what he had been given. Those who multiplied their resources were rewarded with more. The one who only maintained his resources had even that taken away.[8]

It's interesting that in this parable, those who approach their stewardship by embracing their master's trust are given a remarkable invitation: "Enter into the joy of your master" (Matthew 25:21, 23). The one who functions out of fear based on what he "knows"—which, as it turns out, is quite a different perception of the master than that of the other two servants, who focus only on the master's trust in them—is thrown into the darkness where there's "weeping and gnashing of teeth." He doesn't seem to consider the possibility that there *is* such a thing as the joy of the master. The master clearly delights in the servants who value his trust and is angry with the one who perceives him only as "a hard man." In the case of each servant, the parable ends with a very emotional outcome: either the master's joy or the pain of missing out on it.

Think about how this parable might apply to our discussion of the heart of God. Do some people today believe God is a hard master? Of course. Those who struggle to please him with their performance will eventually believe that he's impossible to please—not because he really is, but because they think he's interested in a level of performance that they'll never be able to achieve. That's frustrating, and it crushes a person under the impossible weight of holy perfection.

On the other hand, do some people today believe God has entrusted them with many blessings and resources they can use to serve him? Yes, of course, but perhaps not as many as we think. Note that this parable isn't about tithing; the good servants invested *everything*, not just a tenth. You can't do that unless you feel a certain amount of safety in the Master. No one goes around investing resources in every direction unless they know that the owner of the resources allows risk-takers to lose everything—and that he'll at least be pleased that they tried. You have to know something of the heart of the Master to lay yourself completely on the line. Not many people are able to do that. Only a few have that kind of trust.

And the Master, for his part, clearly delights in that trust. The reward he gives is not only more responsibility but an invitation into his celebration. He's the kind of Master who is willing to put his resources on the line too. He knows all about investing precious things. He even laid his only Son on the line to reap an eternally growing return on his investment. It's his nature to sacrifice everything in hopes of gaining everything back and more. He wants his servants to have that kind of heart, and he rejoices when he finds some who do.

That considered, it's amazing how many people think God prefers to watch us "from a distance," as a popular song once put it, or even to let his anger smolder just a little bit hotter every time we stumble and fall. No matter how much the Christian community talks about God's love, a high percentage of us live as though he's on the verge of giving up on us. We talk about his mercy a lot; we rarely actually embrace it.

As a result, the human race lives with little desire to share God's feelings. Why would we want to be angry most of the time? Or to deal with the strain of constant suffering? Those neuroses mentioned back in chapter 6 result when the deepest needs of the heart are never met. When our big questions of life—Am I loved? Is anyone proud of me? Does anyone even like me? Am I important?—are unanswered because the only one who really knows us also happens to be a hard master, our mind tries to fix things. It starts justifying, rationalizing, questioning, self-sabotaging, overcompensating, preemptively judging self and others, and basically messing us up to the point that the image of God can scarcely be seen anymore. If we don't view God as happy, life is miserable indeed.

We forget that God's dominant source of emotions is his love, and that all others flow out of that. That means that he is ultimately a delighted celebrator, not an irate cop or a depressed loner. Heaven is overflowing with a company of joyful hosts whose "pleasures forevermore" (Psalm 16:11) will increase throughout eternity.[9] That's why C. S. Lewis was able to call joy "the serious business of heaven." Joy is room temperature whenever God is in the room.

FRUIT FROM FEELINGS

When God is perceived as a hard master—either cold and distant or angry and harsh—the result is barrenness. Our lives become like a field that never gets rain, or that only gets the kind of rain that beats down fragile young shoots before they ever develop. We dry up or get pounded. But God's emotions are only hard for those who never respond to the gentle rains of his mercy. There is, in fact, a place of weeping and gnashing of teeth—a place where the joy of heaven is completely missing. But "a tender shoot"[10] already experienced the distance of God on our behalf ("My God, my God, why have you forsaken me?"[11]) as well as the harshness of God's wrath ("He was crushed for our iniquities"[12]). In exchange, we've been given everything we need for a flourishing, abundant life. We've been planted in the fertile soil of love and

God's dominant source of emotions is his love, and all others flow out of that.

acceptance and cultivated in a climate of promised destiny. There's no reason for us to wander an emotional wasteland and miss out on God's joy.

But we do, don't we? Christians who regularly wrestle with discouragement are surprisingly common. A hope lives within us, and we're able to stand firmer in the trials of life than those who don't know God, but many of us don't exactly experience his pleasure. We have a deferred hope, not a daily celebration. When we miss out on his joy, we miss out on his fruitfulness.

I've found that statement to be an inviolable principle in my life, and I'm guessing it's true of you too. When I'm discouraged, I can hardly write anything. It's not that I don't have any ideas or forget how to be industrious. But the "emotivation" just isn't there, and creativity can't flourish in that context. When emotion is absent, people aren't very productive. And when God's emotions are absent, Christians aren't very fruitful.

All of us, however, can relate to the surge of energy that comes with authentic emotions—especially the good ones. When we're full of joy, imagination flows. Like a romantic couple that gets creative in expressing their feelings, fruitfulness just seems to happen. The parallel to our relationship with God is clear. When we know him intimately, sharing his heart and living in his climate of joy, his fruitfulness flows through us. Living "in him" in the way that a branch draws its life from the vine[13] should include the nutritional value of his feelings. The more we become "one" with him, the more we bear his kind of fruit.

God made us that way. It's impossible for us to flourish—or even to survive—without having a vital heart connection with him. In redemption, we have been filled with a Spirit that births love, joy, peace, patience, kindness, and gentleness in us, and who can be grieved and quenched by our hardness of heart. The gospel—the good news—is emotional through and through.

EMOTIONAL MAPPING

If God is emotional and we're created and redeemed to have an empathetic connection with him, how to cultivate that connection becomes a vital question. One of the greatest tools I have found is an approach I call "emotional mapping."

Sometimes the Bible should be read intuitively and empathetically. We do that by absorbing the emotional state of its characters and the emotional impact of its stories. Plenty of emotional language is usually provided, but even when it's not, we can project our own emotions into the written word. There's no law that requires us to read the Bible in monotone with a British accent like they do on audiobooks. Because tone of voice is often undetectable in written language, we're allowed to try out any level of expressiveness when reading the Bible. We can assume more emotion in those words than we normally assume. Placing ourselves in the midst of the action will help us do that.

When we read of Abraham's walk up Mount Moriah to obey God by sacrificing Isaac,[14] for example, it's entirely appropriate to imagine ourselves in his place—to ask how he felt, or how Sarah would have felt as she heard the story later, or how Isaac must have felt on the way back down the mountain, knowing that his father was really going to put a knife through him on the altar.

Considering the emotions of the humans in the story is the first step. But as we do that, we should always end up with our primary focus on the main character: God. What feelings did he have in commanding Abraham to do such a difficult thing? Did he cry with Abraham going up the mountain and rejoice with him coming down? Did he feel the emotions he'd later pour out when he put his own Son on the altar? What peace did God have, knowing that he wasn't going to let Abraham go through with the plan? And, to translate the situation into our own experience, what peace does God have today about our difficult situation, in light of the fact that he already knows how it will end in our joy if we trust him?

We get hints of God's emotions in the text itself—he refers to Isaac as the son "whom you love," clearly sensitive to the heartstrings involved, and fatherly pride oozes out of the approving statements in Genesis 22:16-18 as though it couldn't wait to be expressed. But even beyond specific emotional cues, our knowledge of God from the rest of Scripture gives us enough insight to draw emotional depth from the story.

When we begin to map Scripture not according to plotlines but instead according to emotional responses, the words on the page somehow become more three-dimensional. We begin to feel the peace God has in humanity's most traumatic situations and to focus on the joy that he has promised. We become less subject to the kinds of fleeting emotions God's people felt in the wilderness where they almost constantly complained, and we develop a greater capacity to endure the crises and annoyances we'll face in our lives today. We begin to synchronize with the heartbeat of eternity.

There are many great portions of Scripture to read empathetically—that is, to map emotionally: the life of Jacob or Joseph, the Exodus, the stories of Saul and David, the life of Job, the lives and messages of the prophets, and the Gospels, for a few examples. One of my favorites is Nehemiah.

The Joy of the Lord Is Your Strength

It begins with a man who's completely broken about the state of Jerusalem, its walls still in disrepair many years after Judah's return from captivity. Far away in the capital of Persia, Nehemiah hears a report from his friends in Jerusalem and reacts with the emotions God must have felt for his holy city: "As soon as I heard these words, I sat down and wept and mourned for days, and I continued fasting and praying before the God of heaven" (1:4). That grief leads to one of the most heartfelt prayers recorded in Scripture. It can even be argued that Nehemiah's sadness becomes the catalyst for his obedience. The king notices his demeanor, asks him what is wrong, and, upon Nehemiah's answer, provides him all he needs to go to Jerusalem and rebuild its walls. A pivotal work in God's Kingdom was made possible because one man grieved.

Nehemiah expresses his calling in terms of "what my God had put into my heart to do" (2:12). He understands the principle of feeling like God, and it serves him well throughout his ministry. When Sanballat, an ardent opponent of Judah, hears that the city wall is being rebuilt, "he was angry and greatly enraged, and he jeered at the Jews" (4:1). Along with others, he begins to attack the workmanship and the purposes of the project to demoralize the people. But Nehemiah isn't demoralized, and he encourages the citizens of Jerusalem when their hearts begin to fail. "Do not be afraid of them. Remember the Lord, who is great and awesome" (4:14). When Nehemiah hears of the economic oppression of Jewish laborers at the hand of other Jews, he is "very angry" and exhorts the oppressors to live "in the fear of our God" (5:6, 9).

When their taunting fails to demoralize the Jews, the opponents of Jerusalem try two different modes of attack to stall the work. The first is a mind game. Sanballat, Tobiah, and Geshem, three thorns in the side of God's people, begin lying about Judah's reputation—that its people want to rebel against Persia—and about Nehemiah's motives—that he wants to make himself king. The enemy's deceptions frequently take such a tack, stirring external and internal suspicions simultaneously. Nehemiah's response? "They all wanted to frighten us. . . . But now, O God, strengthen my hands" (6:9).

The second strategy aims at prompting a misguided action. Sanballat and Tobiah hire a "prophet" to tell Nehemiah of an assassination plot against him so he will go into the temple and hide. Nehemiah again is unmoved: "[They] wanted to make me afraid" (6:14).

The wall is finished, and "God put[s] it into [Nehemiah's] heart to assemble the nobles and the officials and the people" (7:5). When Ezra the scribe reads the law to all the people, their response is extremely emotional; they mourn and weep because they realize how they have neglected God's law for generations. But Nehemiah tells them not to mourn—it is a holy feast day, according to the law—and utters the best-known sentence from this book of the Bible: "The joy of the LORD is your strength" (8:10). The priests calm all the people, who then go their way "to make great rejoicing" (8:12). They later go through a season of confession and deep repentance, and then when the wall is dedicated, they celebrate "with gladness, with thanksgivings and with singing, with cymbals, harps, and lyres. . . . They offered great sacrifices that day and rejoiced, *for God had made them rejoice with great joy*; the women and children also rejoiced. And the joy of Jerusalem was heard far away" (12:27, 43, italics added).

That celebration would make a great ending to the book, but the spiritual transformation of God's people isn't complete. There are still pagan influences in the city that corrupt God's remnant from within the walls. On three occasions, Nehemiah's outrage prompts him to institute further reforms. When he discovers that a chamber in the temple courts has been set apart and furnished for Tobiah, one of the Jews' most persistent enemies, he is "very angry," and throws "all the household furniture of Tobiah out of the chamber," and orders its cleansing (13:8-9). When he sees Judeans treading winepresses on the Sabbath, breaking the law, he boldly and angrily confronts the nobles and begins shutting the doors of the city every Sabbath so no one can go work in the fields. And when he encounters Jews who have married pagan women and have children who can speak foreign languages but not Hebrew, he reacts most violently. "I confronted them and cursed them and beat some of them and pulled out their hair. And I made them take oath in the name of God" (13:25).

That last reaction doesn't usually make it into leadership studies based on Nehemiah's life, and I'm not sure his outward reaction is necessarily in line with God's will. But the emotion behind it certainly fits God's heart. God has allowed this nation to be taken into captivity because of idolatrous practices and rebellion against him, and in this time of restoration many of its people are falling into the same traps that led them into judgment in the first place. Surely God's anger burns against such foolishness. Therefore, so does Nehemiah's.

In fact, if we focus exclusively on God's emotions in this book, we see them showing up in the responses of his people, particularly in Nehemiah himself. There's a heart of love in this character that produces deep sadness over failure and sin, joyful exuberance over the Kingdom of God's establishment, and jealous anger over unfaithfulness and apathy. Sounds a lot like God, doesn't it?

That's the emotional plot of one book of the Bible. It begins with grief that is based on truth and leads to action; it reports the firm stand God's people take against discouragement and deception; it plumbs the depths of repentance and soars to the heights of celebration; and it ends with an angry determination to abstain from every form of evil. And, at the most pivotal, climactic moment in the story, it reminds us that the *joy* of the Lord is our strength. Not the mental understanding, not the sterile obedience, but the joy. Why? Because that's the climate of heaven and the environment in which understanding and obedience flourish.

Do you see how emotional the story line is? There's a lot of truth to glean out of Nehemiah, as well as many action points. But if that's all we get from it, the desire God has to share his feelings with us eludes us. We miss out on understanding who he is. When we read the Bible and review our daily circumstances with an eye for the emotions of God, however, we begin to understand him, and he delights in our newfound understanding. He shares his heart with us more and more because he knows we won't miss it. Intimacy thrives.

When we beat with God's heartbeat, he gives us his dreams and empowers us to fulfill them.

The result of intimacy with God is the same as the result of intimacy in marriage: a fulfilling relationship, love and joy, selflessness, shared happiness in other areas of life, and, last but not least, children. This is where Christians become fruitful. When we beat with God's heartbeat, he gives us his dreams and empowers us to fulfill them. We go about his mission with enthusiasm and confidence because we know he's right there with us. His mission is our mission. Our passions are his passions. This unity of spirit is, to a large degree, what Jesus was talking about when he spoke of our abiding in him and him in us. Prayers get answered in that kind of relationship. Plans get accomplished. New disciples are won by the kindness of God that leads to repentance[15] rather than the harshness of God that usually does not. Life becomes a relationship rather than an activity. We become one with God not only in name but in practice.

Many Christians try to get to this point by understanding and doing—by engaging only the mind and the will and assuming that the Spirit is somehow, though imperceptibly, involved in the process. But that won't get anyone closer to God. It will get us closer to the things of God, immersing us in Kingdom activities and relationships, but it won't keep us from feeling alienated from his Spirit. In order to truly fellowship with him, we need to do so at a deep emotional level.

A GREAT PRAYER

How can we do that? Ask. That's it—or at least the most important part of it. It doesn't begin with more understanding or more activity, though both will result. It begins with a request.

Think about it. How would you respond if someone you love came to you and said something like this? "I really want to get to know you better. Will you share your heart with me? I want us to be closer." If an acquaintance you cared little about asked you that, you might not be very motivated to invest more time in that relationship—especially if your time is spread pretty thin already. But if a spouse, a child, a sibling, or a close friend came to you with a hunger to know you more, it would move you. You'd be touched. And you'd be drawn to that person.

That's how it is with God. He responds to hunger. In fact, there's plenty of scriptural evidence that he responds to hunger more than he does to your attempts to be a good person whom he'll be proud of. Parents, bosses, teachers, and anyone in a position of authority is pleased with those who do well, but compellingly drawn to those with a desire to relate to them. That's the nature of God's heart too.

I've found that the following prayer taps into God's heart in a unique way and virtually always gets answered. The answer may be imperceptible at first, but when you look back over a few weeks or months, there will be no denying that he honored your request. You will experience more love, more joy, and, alas, more pain in the process. But these will not be random emotions. They'll be his.

Here's my prayer: *Today, Lord, I want to feel your feelings, to think your thoughts, to have your heart, to let your Spirit flow through me, to breathe the air of heaven, to feel the warmth of your love. Whatever comes into me or out of me, I'll trust that it's from you unless you clearly show me that it isn't. I want whatever I do to be the natural outflow of your heart within me, and wherever my heart is not in line with yours, I pray that you would let me know. I want your Spirit completely—your heart, your mind, and your will—inside of me where we can fellowship, not outside of me where I have to blindly obey and guess about who you are. I want love between you and me to be alive and powerful, and I'm asking that you make it so. Amen.*

Can you imagine God *not* answering that prayer? I can't either. Just a few days ago, in fact, I faced a complicated situation and asked, "Lord, where's your heart in all this? How do you feel about it?" Hours later, someone reacting to a similar situation demonstrated profound grief about the problem and hope for the solution. That inner impulse—the subjective one so many are afraid of—clearly said, "Chris, that's how I feel about it." That's one story among many, more than enough to convince me God is eager to answer that prayer. It's inconceivable that he would go to the excruciating trouble of redemption over the course of millennia, culminating with the death of his Son on the cross, to restore a broken relationship and fill us with his Spirit—and then ignore a sincere request for that relationship to be everything it was meant to be. God is neither unfeeling or illogical. This prayer, I would venture to say, always gets answered.

I'm convinced that you'll find that to be true in your experience, and the result will be life-changing. You can become a David or a Nehemiah, winning great victories in his strength and becoming more in tune with him than you've ever been.

If you feel any emptiness in your walk with the Lord, if you've always wondered if you're missing something or if an in-depth intimacy with him is really possible, pray for his heart to become your heart. Speak the language of lovers who always want a closer, deeper relationship. Try reading the Bible with an eye on the emotions that flow out of its pages—especially the emotions of the Source of the Word. Ask God to stir up his heart and his mind within you—to feel as he feels and to think as he thinks. Then notice what happens. Over time, you'll find yourself feeling godly feelings, growing closer to him, experiencing an abundant life, and hearing his voice as he writes it on your heart. You might actually begin to feel that you can be yourself in front of God and everybody. You'll also find yourself intuitively doing his will, though it may seem like your will because yours and his are so tightly intertwined. In many ways, perhaps as never before, you'll find yourself conformed to the image of Christ—in sync with the God who made you to be close to his heart.

If you've always wondered if in-depth intimacy with God is really possible, pray for his heart to become your heart.

CONCLUSION[1]

THE YOUNG MAN'S hand shook as he set the cup in front of her. The moment of decision had come. He had been waiting his whole life for this day, and all his dreams and desires were wrapped up in it. It had taken all of his resources and all of his courage to arrange for this crucial moment.

He had help, of course. His father had counseled him, dutifully walked to the nearby town in order to get to know her parents, and talked with them about the merits of this match. The parents discussed the details of where the son would live, of how he would provide for their daughter, and, of course, of the price they would require. But only the bride herself could pick up this cup of wine and drink it. Only she could agree to become his wife.

Seconds after he placed the wine on the table—though it seemed to him like hours—she reached out, smiled nervously, lifted it to her mouth, and drank. Her gesture said "Yes!" louder than any shout from a mountaintop. Yes, his dream would be fulfilled. Yes, she would marry him.

The young man's anxiety melted away, and unbridled joy took its place. This was a done deal, as binding as the marriage ceremony itself. All that was left for him to do was to go home with his parents and prepare a room in their house, a place where he and the delight of his heart could live together and enjoy the fruits of their marriage.

As the families celebrated and chattered excitedly about a future full of promise, she leaned toward him discreetly. "When can we have the wedding?" she whispered.

"I don't know," he whispered back to her. "It's up to my father. Whenever he tells me the house is good enough for us to live in, I'll come for you."

Soon, he hoped. He would work hard to prepare a place as quickly as he could. Then he and his friends, his groomsmen, would come back to her town blowing happily on a *shofar*, a ram's horn, to alert her of his arrival. When she heard the blast of the trumpet, it would be time for the wedding.

In the meantime, she would wear a veil to let the whole world know that someone had chosen her, and she would spend her days beautifying her appearance and purifying her heart. She would also keep a lamp by her bed, just in case he returned during the night. Her bridesmaids would do the same because, after all, one never knows when an eager groom is going to come for his bride. No degree of darkness can keep him away.

GOD'S ENGAGEMENT

This scene has many of the elements of a typical Jewish engagement in the time of Jesus. Many of those elements came from the symbolism of Sinai. The deliverance of Israel involved a covenant of blood as a bride price[2] and included all the terms of a marriage: the generous provision of the husband,[3] the purification of the bride,[4] his expectations for the marriage,[5] the fire of his lamp descending on the mountain,[6] and the blast of his shofar.[7] In the centuries since, rabbis have taught that the Ten Commandments were an engagement contract. God had chosen a bride. Even today, Jews drink a cup of wine at Passover to accept his proposal.

Jesus, the exact imprint of God, clearly identified with many of these customs. He set a cup of wine before his disciples and asked them to drink it. He spilled his own blood as a bride price—not grudgingly, but for the joy it would bring. Before he left his disciples, he told them that he was going away to prepare a place for them in his Father's house, but he would surely return and receive them to himself.[8] He told his disciples that he would come again with all his angels and the blast of a trumpet.[9] The Kingdom of Heaven would be like bridesmaids who went out to meet the Bridegroom, but no one knew when that would be.[10] Even he didn't know the day or the hour; the time was completely in his Father's hands.[11] And the ultimate celebration would be like a wedding feast that a king gives for his son.[12]

New Testament writers pick up on the theme, as Paul tells the Corinthians that he has betrothed them to Jesus and wants them to be pure for the wedding.[13] And if we had any doubt about where history is headed, Revelation makes it clear: "The wedding of the Lamb has come, and his bride has made herself ready. Fine linen, bright and clean, was given her to wear" (Revelation 19:7-8, NIV). All of heaven's hallelujahs will crescendo when the ceremony comes and the wedding feast has begun.

Scripture resounds with wedding theology, from the Garden of Eden to the City of God. In Genesis, one man becomes two people, and then two people become "one flesh," and this, Paul says, is the mystery of Christ and his church.[14] About halfway between Genesis and Revelation, the Song of Songs describes how Solomon and his beloved explore each other fully. Though the words make us blush, many Jewish and Christian theologians alike have long seen it as an allegory of God and his people. From the first "be fruitful and multiply" to the marriage supper of the Lamb, the Bridegroom seeks a bride.

BEFORE THE WEDDING

We live in that time of engagement. If we've drunk his proposal cup, our marriage contract is as binding as the wedding ceremony itself. This betrothal period is a time of transformation: We eagerly anticipate the return of the Bridegroom, and he eagerly anticipates our enthusiastic greeting when he comes. We begin to dream not in general terms of our wedding day, but of the life we'll have as a couple and what we'll do together for the rest of time. We start practicing our new signature with our new last name, trying out different options and letting the sound of our new identity roll off our tongues for all to hear. We beautify ourselves even now, because we want his face to light up when we walk the aisle.

We have no need now to suppress the things we feel or to ignore the hold they have on our hearts. We don't let our thoughts wander to possibilities of other romances, envisioning what it would be like to live in union with strangers. No, we let our emotions invest even further in the relationship at hand, because now we know it won't end in disappointment. We're free to dream, free to love, and free to let our feelings merge with the heartbeat of the one we love. The outward signs of betrothal have linked us to him forever, and the internal swells of passion will no longer need restraint. We live our lives with one focus: the knitting together of two hearts in love.

It would be sad for that focus to get lost in the shuffle of planning the wedding. It would also signify an enormous problem if we find ourselves constantly reminding ourselves that a wedding is coming and forcing our hearts to return to the relationship at hand. If it's a strain to remember that we're betrothed and we have to surround ourselves with people who prompt us to do the things we're supposed to do, something's wrong. If we keep having to tell ourselves, "It's an arrangement, not a romance; it's an agreement, not an emotion," we're missing out on the very purpose of the marriage itself. If we're engaged but our hearts are not, our minds are fighting an uphill battle that they will probably lose.

But real relationships of love don't normally have those problems. They're filled with anticipation, and all activity is based on our eager expectations of what's to come. We get ready for the wedding not just because it's the right thing to do, but because we want to be ready for it. We figure out what we should wear and how we should act because of what's in our hearts. Our thoughts and our actions are highly persuaded by what we feel, and no one would expect otherwise.

This betrothal period is a time of transformation: We eagerly anticipate the return of the Bridegroom, and he eagerly anticipates our enthusiastic greeting when he comes.

During this time, our devotion deepens and our Bridegroom's dreams and goals become a part of us. We will plan with him, work with him, cry with him, laugh with him, and become one with him. That's what marriage is. It brings two souls together in a unity of spirit and heart and mind and body. It's not a system of education, though we'll learn much. It's not a place of employment, though we'll do a lot. It's a sharing of hearts, and when the emotional union is flourishing, the rest seems to take care of itself.

That's what discipleship is: the betrothal of the Bridegroom and the bride. It involves new understanding and plenty of lifestyle adjustments, but at its core it's a heart connection that fuels everything else around us. There's a celebration at the heart of the universe, and we're invited to be in it. Not to learn of it, not to act like we *should* be celebrating whether or not we're really on board with it, but to enjoy it and let it become the basis of all we think and do. We've been invited to a ball.

BACK TO THE PROPOSAL

The young man and his future bride sit together and watch the festivities of their two families. Their hearts are still racing: hers because he asked, and his because she said yes. And though they don't know it yet, that quickened pulse is synchronizing between the two of them. It's speeding along at the same pace and developing the same rhythm. And as the families eat and drink and laugh about their happiness and share their dreams for their children, this young bridegroom leans over to his betrothed and asks her one more question.

Would you like to dance?

NOTES

CHAPTER 1
1. *A River Runs Through It*, Columbia Pictures, 1992.
2. *Sense and Sensibility*, Columbia Pictures, 1995. Though the film follows the plot of the novel very closely, a few details vary between them. The illustration in this chapter is drawn from the specifics of the film.
3. Isaiah 55:8-9
4. Hebrews 1:3; Colossians 1:15
5. 2 Corinthians 5:21
6. Hebrews 5:7
7. Exodus 34:14
8. Deuteronomy 6:15; Psalm 79:5; Zechariah 8:2, NIV
9. Malachi 3:6; Hebrews 13:8
10. Exodus 32:14; Isaiah 38:5
11. This is also expressed well in the Westminster Shorter Catechism: "to glorify God and *enjoy* him forever" (italics added).
12. Revelation 2:4-5. The result of their repentance is to "do the works you did at first," which seems like a very action-oriented instruction. But the rest of Scripture is emphatic that works with no heart behind them are repulsive to God. Love has to be the motivation.
13. Revelation 3:1-3
14. Revelation 3:15-16

CHAPTER 2
1. Actually, they tied for the honor of being the first last-place team to go to the Series. The team they lost to in seven games was the Minnesota Twins, who also had made it to the World Series after having been worst in their division the previous year.
2. Matthew 18:3-4; Mark 10:15; Luke 18:17
3. I am not using this analysis of our being in a Greek rational way. Greek philosophy (as well as the doctrines of many Christians) compartmentalized the personality in ways the Bible never does. In Scripture, human beings are integrated wholes: body, soul, and spirit are one ultimately inseparable unit, which is why the resurrection is so critical. The Bible does not teach a soul-only, exclusively spiritual salvation. God's re-creation of the new earth maintains physical elements.

   For the purposes of this book, however, I use the terms *mind*, *will*, and *emotions* not as compartments but as descriptions of aspects we all know we have. Whatever you believe the human soul to be, we can all agree that we have minds that rationally process information; that we have the capacity to act by force of the will; and that we have feelings that often but not always correlate directly with the information at hand.
4. I introduced this illustration in my book *Creative Prayer* (Multnomah, 2006).

5. 2 Corinthians 3:6
6. Romans 12:2
7. Ezekiel 36:26
8. Jesus is quoting Isaiah 29:13.
9. James 2:19
10. There has been a revival of sorts of the battle between Gnosticism and orthodox Christianity. That battle is the core of the controversies surrounding the Gospel of Judas, the Gospel of Thomas, and the wildly popular book *The DaVinci Code*.
11. *Fiddler on the Roof*, United Artists, 1971.
12. Luke 1:34, NASB
13. 1 Corinthians 2:11-16
14. Matthew 22:37
15. It's important to note that the heart, as the word is used in Scripture, doesn't always apply only to emotions, as it usually does when we use the word in today's English. Sometimes it specifically relates to feelings; other times it's more comprehensive, referring also to thoughts and personality without excluding emotions. In other words, it often refers to the entire inner person, emotions and all. But according to *Nave's Topical Bible*, it usually refers to the seat of our affections, just as it often does in modern English. That's the sense in which I'm using it in this book, referring to the biblical term only when the original text implies emotions.

CHAPTER 3

1. 1 John 4:8, 16
2. "The Four Spiritual Laws," a Campus Crusade for Christ booklet
3. John 5:20
4. John 16:27
5. John 11:3
6. Exodus 19–20
7. Exodus 34:14
8. Satan's willful self-centeredness is the subject behind the symbolism in Isaiah 14:13-14.
9. James 4:6; 1 Peter 5:5
10. As in the Song of Songs
11. Ephesians 5:31-32
12. Leviticus 20:13; Deuteronomy 23:18; 24:4
13. Psalm 31:5; Isaiah 65:16, NIV
14. Deuteronomy 25:16
15. Jeremiah 29:11
16. Psalm 101:5
17. John 17:11-21
18. Numbers 11:1
19. Numbers 14:26-32
20. Amos 5:21
21. Isaiah 30:18
22. Ezekiel 9:9-10
23. Malachi 2:16
24. Exodus 34:6, for one well-known example.
25. The examples of God's wrath in the prophetic books are numerous, but for a good representative taste of it, try Ezekiel 7. An excerpt: "I am about to pour out my wrath on

you and spend my anger against you; I will judge you according to your conduct and repay you for all your detestable practices. I will not look on you with pity or spare you; I will repay you in accordance with your conduct and the detestable practices among you. Then you will know that it is I the LORD who strikes the blow" (vv. 8-9, NIV).

26. Matthew 23:37
27. Ephesians 4:30
28. 2 Kings 19:31; Isaiah 9:7; 37:32
29. Isaiah 42:13
30. Isaiah 59:17
31. Ezekiel 5:13; 38:19; Zephaniah 3:8
32. John 2:17
33. Zephaniah 3:8
34. 2 Samuel 22:20; Psalm 18:19
35. 1 Kings 10:9
36. Psalm 149:4
37. Proverbs 12:22
38. Jeremiah 9:24
39. Exodus 34:6, NIV
40. Exodus 34:5
41. Exodus 33:20
42. The one exception is fear that is based on a known rift between us and our God. The fear of the Lord is legitimate and necessary, and the fear that results from rebelling against him is warranted. It's a terrifying thing to fall into the hands of the living God (Hebrews 10:31). But for the purposes of this discussion, fear is anxiety or cowardice about present circumstances or our future—the emotions we wouldn't have if we saw things as God sees them.
43. Amos 5:15

CHAPTER 4

1. By "mountaintop experience," I'm referring to one of those emotionally charged moments in which the Spirit is "felt" and truth seems to have a more powerful impact than at other times. They are moving experiences during which people often make landmark decisions.
2. The rebellion of Korah and its aftermath, as recorded in Numbers 16–17, was essentially a charge that because life in the Promised Land was not yet a reality, Moses must not have been getting his messages from God—at least not in any way distinguishable from the rest of the Israelites (16:3, 28)—and his works were his, not God's (16:30, 41). Their objective observations did not line up with his subjective revelations (16:14). In powerful terms, God authenticated Moses as his servant and Aaron as Israel's priest.
3. Isaiah 6:5-8
4. Daniel 7:15, 28; 8:27; 10:2, 7-11.
5. E. Y. Harburg, "If I Only Had a Brain," *The Wizard of Oz: Original Motion Picture Soundtrack*, 1939.
6. Consider how many of the fruits of the Spirit listed in Galatians 5:22-23 are emotionally laden terms: love, joy, peace, patience, kindness, and gentleness.
7. Numbers 25:1-13. The word *jealous* is emphasized by its fourfold repetition in the space of two sentences in verses 11-13.
8. This research is explained and demonstrated with many more examples in Steven

Strogatz's fascinating book *Sync: The Emerging Science of Spontaneous Order* (New York: Penguin Books, 2004). Strogatz is a mathematics professor at Cornell University.

9. I find that obedience can either have an emotional impetus or be a matter of raw willpower. Willpower obedience is often motivated by guilt, whereas emotion-inspired obedience is usually a desire for the joy that obedience brings.
10. If you find yourself in this latter situation, go ahead and obey the verse anyway. That's better than disobeying because you didn't feel like obeying. But let your heart alert you to the fact that you aren't in sync with God on that instruction, and ask him to give you his heart on the subject.
11. 2 Corinthians 3:6
12. Deuteronomy 32:10
13. Philippians 3:10

CHAPTER 5
1. Aldous Huxley, *Brave New World*, 1932.
2. Isaiah 20
3. Ezekiel 4:1-8
4. Hosea 1
5. Genesis 22
6. John 15:11
7. John 17:13
8. Hebrews 5:7
9. Hebrews 12:2
10. In fact, John Calvin's first literary work, completed before his conversion to reformed Christianity, was a commentary on Seneca's political treatise *De Clementia*—"On Clemency."
11. This illustration is found in Campus Crusade's "Four Spiritual Laws" tract as well as numerous other places.
12. Matthew 13:5-6
13. Martin Luther, "Preface to Complete Edition of Luther's Latin Writings," *Luther's Works*, vol. 34, *Career of the Reformer IV* (St. Louis: Concordia Publishing House, 1960), 336–337.
14. American Passages: A Literary Survey, "Jonathan Edwards," *Unit 4: Spirit of Nationalism*, Annenberg Media, http://www.learner .org/amerpass/unit04/authors-3.html.
15. Matthew 11:30
16. 2 Corinthians 3:17

CHAPTER 6
1. Gordon-Conwell Theological Seminary research statistics
2. Though I've discussed depression and anxiety in emotional terms elsewhere, they are emotions that come about from a misperception of facts. They are simultaneously mind and heart issues.
3. George Wald, *Frontiers of Modern Biology on Theories of Origin of Life*, (New York: Houghton Mifflin, 1972).
4. These reversals in the scientific community were part of David Barton's June 2007 testimony to the U.S. Senate on the evangelical community's opinions of the global warming debate. His testimony, with full documentation, can be found online at www.

christianworldviewnetwork.com/article.php/2415/David_Barton. My point in citing
these inconsistencies in scientific opinion is not to indicate my position on any of them
but simply to demonstrate that society's minds don't always know what they think they
know. Intellectual "consensus" is very often unreliable.

5. 1 Corinthians 2:14
6. John 9:18-19
7. Luke 24:13-35
8. Luke 24:38
9. Luke 24:45
10. 1 Corinthians 2:14-16
11. Paul Simon and Art Garfunkel, "I Am a Rock," *The Sound of Silence*, 1966.
12. My experience with Buddhism is drawn from the Theravadan strain practiced in many
parts of Southeast Asia. There are many different branches of the religion, and some
do not exactly fit the description I'm giving here.
13. Philippians 3:10

CHAPTER 7

1. Star Trek II: *The Wrath of Khan*, Paramount Pictures, 1982.
2. I also use this illustration and line of reasoning in *Creative Prayer* (Multnomah, 2006).
3. Psalm 16:11, for one example. There's ample evidence of God's pleasure in Scripture,
as in Matthew 11:26 and Ephesians 1:9, NIV.
4. Star Wars: Episode V—*The Empire Strikes Back*, Twentieth Century-Fox Film
Corporation,1980.
5. Italics added in all quotations in this paragraph.
6. Matthew 12:34; 23:33
7. Matthew 23:13-36; Luke 11:37-54
8. Luke 11:45
9. Ephesians 4:26
10. Matthew 5:1-12
11. Philippians 1:18-26
12. Philippians 1:9, 27 (with 28); 2:2; 4:7
13. Philippians 2:5; 3:4, 15, 19; 4:8
14. 2 Corinthians 1:3-7
15. 2 Corinthians 9:7
16. 2 Corinthians 11:2
17. 2 Corinthians 12:1-7
18. Acts 2:12, 43; and every other time people marveled at a work of God and then
received an explanation afterward.

CHAPTER 8

1. Jesus did warn his followers that many deceivers would come in his name doing signs
and wonders (Matthew 24:5, 24). This warning, however, is meant to caution us that
not everything supernatural is from God. It is not teaching us to explain miracles in
naturalistic terms until proven otherwise. Whenever people encountered a miracle in
the Gospels, they faced a choice. Those who believed and rejoiced were commended;
those who questioned whether a miracle really happened were rebuked.
2. Mark 16:14
3. Acts 17:32, for example

4. Acts 23:6
5. Matthew 5:11-12
6. 2 Timothy 3:12
7. 1 Corinthians 1:25
8. Mark 8:38
9. *Forrest Gump*, Paramount Pictures, 1994.
10. This is the opposite of what many people teach—"Do what's right and the feelings will follow." Paul's exhortation says, in effect, "Feel what's right and the doing will follow." It isn't that one is right and the other wrong. They are both true to a degree, and each element of our personalities is meant to complement (and often lead) the others.
11. This isn't the "resentment" kind of bitterness but a grievous anger that troubles one's spirit.
12. Psalm 30:11; Jeremiah 31:13
13. John 14:27; Philippians 4:6-7
14. 1 Samuel 17
15. 1 Samuel 13:11-14
16. 1 Samuel 14:24-46
17. 1 Samuel 18:10-11, among others
18. 1 Samuel 16:7
19. Acts 9:7
20. 2 Corinthians 12:1-7
21. Amos's observation in 3:7 about God sharing his secrets was specific to prophets in his day, but, in light of New Testament spiritual gifts, is much more widely applicable today. (Paul's desire and expectation as recorded in 1 Corinthians 14:1-5 is that all of God's people would be able to prophesy.)
22. Jonah 4:10-11

CHAPTER 9
1. Exodus 34:6-7
2. Genesis 15:2-3
3. Genesis 15:1
4. 2 Samuel 11
5. 1 Samuel 1
6. Jonah 2:7
7. A similar incident appears in Judges 11:29-39 when Jephthah makes a deal with God: If God delivers the Ammonites into his hands, he will sacrifice the first thing he sees coming out of his doorway when he returns. When his daughter, an only child, comes out dancing and celebrating with tambourines upon his arrival, he cries out in anguish for what he has promised. But he keeps his vow, eventually sacrificing his beloved child.
8. Isaiah 20
9. Ezekiel 4:9-17

CHAPTER 10
1. Genesis 18:23-32
2. Isaiah 22:12
3. Joseph Chilton Pearce, *Evolution's End* (New York: HarperCollins, 1992), quoted in Cori Young, "Child Development," natural-humor-medicine.com, http://www.natural-humor-medicine.com/child-development.html (accessed July 2, 2007). Though Pearce draws

evolutionary conclusions, the evidence is applicable regardless of one's beliefs about our origins. For a Christian, this dynamic is an example of the wisdom of God woven into his creation.

4. Ibid.
5. Ephesians 3:20; 1 Corinthians 2:9
6. John 10:10
7. Psalm 16:11
8. Matthew 25:14-30
9. Isaiah 9:7 says that there will be no end to the Messiah's reign. It will always be expanding, giving all in his Kingdom reason to perpetually rejoice.
10. Isaiah 53:2, NIV
11. Mark 15:34
12. Isaiah 53:5
13. John 15:4-5
14. Genesis 22
15. Romans 2:4

CONCLUSION
1. This is adapted from an article I wrote for *OnMission* magazine.
2. Exodus 12:13
3. Exodus 19:4; 20:2
4. Exodus 19:5-6
5. Exodus 20:3-17
6. Exodus 20:18
7. Exodus 19:13
8. John 14:1-3
9. Matthew 24:30-31
10. Matthew 25:1-13
11. Matthew 24:36
12. Matthew 22:2
13. 2 Corinthians 11:2
14. Ephesians 5:32

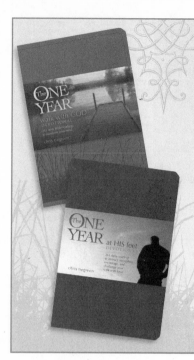